change your life with

earth
magic

change your life with

earth
magic

The ancient chinese art of harmonising yourself
with the energies of the earth and the heavens

——— GARY QUELCH ———

foulsham

LONDON • NEW YORK • TORONTO • SYDNEY

foulsham

The Publishing House, Bennetts Close, Cippenham,
Slough, Berkshire SL1 5AP, England

ISBN 0-572-02598-X

Printed in Great Britain by St Edmundsbury Press, Bury St Edmunds, Suffolk

Contents

風水

Introduction	7
The Five Elements	9
Positive Energy in the Home	13
Understanding the Portents	18
The Directions and the Elements	24
Introducing the Flying Stars	27
More About the Flying Stars	33
Positive Energy at Work	39
Introducing the Eight Trigrams	42
The Arrangements of the Trigrams	46
The Elements and Successful Business	51
Your Pillars of Destiny	55
Calculating Your Day Pillar	57
Calculating your Year Pillar	61
Calculating your Month Pillar	63
Calculating your Hour Pillar	65
Constructing a Chart for Your Pillars	67
Evaluating the Strength of Your Personal Element	69
Personal Feng Shui in the Home	73
Water People at Home	75
Wood People at Home	80
Fire People at Home	85
Earth People at Home	90
Metal People at Home	95
Personal Feng Shui for Business	100

Water People at Work   101

Wood People at Work   104

Fire People at Work   107

Earth People at Work   110

Metal People at Work   113

The House of Spouse   116

Relationships for Yang Water People   119

Relationships for Yin Water People   122

Relationships for Yang Wood People   125

Relationships for Yin Wood People   128

Relationships for Yang Fire People   131

Relationships for Yin Fire People   134

Relationships for Yang Earth People   137

Relationships for Yin Earth People   140

Relationships for Yang Metal People   143

Relationships for Yin Metal People   146

Calculating the Fate Cycles   149

How to Use Your Fate Cycles   153

Index   157

Introduction

風水

Although the Chinese have understood the inter-relationship of the energies in the universe for thousands of years, the interest in oriental philosophy is a recent phenomenon in the West, but one that has captured the imagination of millions. In particular, to us in the West, the increased interest in – and to a lesser extent understanding of – feng shui has brought new insights into how we relate to the life energies around us. The fact that it offers constructive ways to change life for the better strikes a chord with the needs of those of us living at the turn of the new millennium. From Hong Kong to Hollywood, everyone has been talking about feng shui, ch'i energy and flying stars, schools have opened, hundreds of books have been published on the subject, and personal consultants have sprung up all over the place, offering consultations that put the principles of Chinese thought into practice in an individual context.

But there's a downside. True feng shui, as it is practised in China, is a highly complex and ancient art, which takes a lifetime to master. Unfortunately, we are too often guilty of wanting a quick fix, and in trying to understand and absorb its concepts quickly, so that we can put its tenets into practice for our own advantage, there has been a lot of over-simplification. You could never encompass Western astrology in a few pages of a magazine article, but there has been a general tendency to think that we can do this with feng shui.

Sometimes, this means that the information we are given is incomplete, unclear or even contradictory. Many people have found that the more they learn, the more confused they become. For example, people who have read a little about feng shui have probably heard that it is often categorised as Form School, Compass School and Black Hat School; but what do these terms mean and do they help to make things clearer – or confuse the issue even more? In fact, there are many different styles within each of these schools, so without considerable knowledge before they make their choice, it is impossible for anyone really to understand how to select a consultant or choose a school.

So how is this book different? And how will it solve the problem?

It will do so simply by looking at feng shui in a more traditional light by going right back to the authentic traditional Chinese principles employed by many of the masters in Hong Kong and Taiwan. Although this book offers a simple and practical approach, I hope that if I introduce and explain some of the core concepts that make up traditional Chinese thought, my readers will no longer be confused, and that the conflicting knowledge they may have already gained will fall into a logical order.

There is a lot more to implementing feng shui than the popular method of working out your *kua* number and determining your favourable directions would suggest. In fact, the Chinese masters do not use 'wealth corners', 'relationship corners' or any of the other 'corners' so popular in Western practice. But by working out your personal element through the traditional method given in this book, understanding how different calculations apply to different areas of your home, and applying this knowledge in a simple way, you will be tuning into authentic Chinese understanding, which I feel has a lot more to offer you in terms of changing your life for the better, including improving your relationships and your chances of financial success. It is important to realise that, contrary to Western popular belief, feng shui is not only to be applied to physical areas such as your home and workplace, but also to your personal and emotional life. If you want to encourage helpful people in your life, you cannot simply stimulate an area of your home, you have first to become a helpful person.

Because there are so many inter-relating aspects of the subject, this book takes a layered approach, giving you an understanding of the simpler concepts first, before delving more deeply into traditional, authentic Chinese feng shui.

Another aspect of feng shui that has received little coverage in the West is the element of luck. Because of its Western connotations, it is a term that does not fully express its importance in Chinese thought, but we all know and use expressions such as 'having a run of bad luck' and 'being on a lucky streak', and these give us some idea of how we can put these principles to good use. As the universal energies ebb and flow, so does the way in which we, as individuals, relate to them, so sometimes we will find things easier to achieve, and work or relationships become more productive. Learning when these good times are likely to come and how we can make the best use of them is crucial to feng shui, as is discovering how to ride out the less auspicious times.

With this book, you will be able to look at the different parts of your life with a new perspective, and begin truly to gain some insight into Chinese metaphysics.

The Five Elements

風水

As a starting point, let's look at the most common Western definition of feng shui. It is usually translated as 'wind and water', because in the West we have focused on the aspect of the subject concerned with the placement of houses and objects in relation to their surroundings.

In Hong Kong, however, feng shui is also known in Cantonese as *ham yu*, which means 'looking up at Heaven and looking down at Earth', and in Taiwan, where Mandarin is spoken, it is also known as *k'an yu*, which means 'studying the mountains and the valleys'. Both of these provide a clearer insight into the meaning, because what we are going to discuss in this book is really the study of how we interact with the forces or energies of Heaven and Earth, known as *ch'i*.

Feng shui is the art of 'going with the flow', of being in harmony with yourself, your loved ones and your environment, and it is based on the same ancient principles as Chinese medicine. It is not just about having your door facing in the right direction or placing flowers in an auspicious position in a room; it is about how we all form a coherent whole with the environment, and it is up to us to be in harmony with the energies in that environment in order to make the best of our lives and those around us.

Chinese metaphysics expresses everything in terms of the elements – from buildings and directions to people and emotions. As feng shui is the study of the interaction of these elements, it can be said to give us a metaphysical view of ourselves and our environment.

These elements, along with the principles of *yin* and *yang*, form the building blocks of all the Chinese sciences, including medicine, acupuncture, astrology and, of course, feng shui. Unlike the Greeks – who referred to the four elements of Air, Water, Fire and Earth – the Chinese define the elements as Wood, Fire, Earth, Metal and Water.

Although they are commonly called elements, it is better to think of them as 'expressions' used to define a type of energy, or as the Chinese call it, ch'i. Like everything else, ch'i can come in many different forms and is not always good. It can also be influenced by anything, even inanimate objects. One of the functions of the feng shui master is to determine the nature of ch'i at any given place and time.

Water energy is cleansing and refreshing and its purpose is renewal. Wood energy is strong and flexible, with the qualities of growth, creation and nourishment. Fire energy is invigorating and stimulating. Earth energy is supportive and reliable. Metal energy is strong and versatile.

The five Chinese elements all work in different ways and relate to each other in a continuous cycle in which they generate, support, weaken, control or destroy each other. In simple terms, this is demonstrated in the generative and destructive cycles. In the generative cycle, Wood is said to generate Fire, which generates Earth, which in turn is said to generate Metal, which generates Water, which then generates Wood.

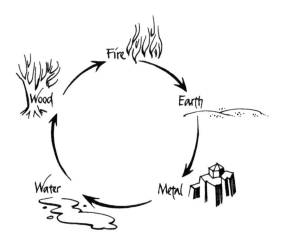

In the destructive cycle, Wood is said to destroy Earth, which destroys Water, which destroys Fire, which in turn destroys Metal, which destroys Wood.

However, understanding these cycles is not enough to give us a full understanding of how these elements work because, as in all matters Chinese, things are more complex when looked at in depth. To have a better understanding of the interaction of the elements, it is important to appreciate how the elements relate to the principles of yin and yang. All ch'i energy is qualified as yin or yang, the complementary yet opposing forces which permeate the universe. Each element can therefore be either yin or yang.

Yang is a positive energy, warm, light and creative. It is associated with the male principle, mountains and summer. Yin is the ultimate contrast: the dark, feminine, quiet and nourishing energy.

In the destructive cycle, Wood is said to be 'destroyed' by Metal. However, yang Wood is said to benefit from the support of yin Metal. This can be explained by the fact that we can only really utilise Wood with the help of Metal, which enables Wood to be transformed into many useful objects. Another good example of this is the relationship between Fire and Water, because the fact that Water is said to 'destroy' Fire only presents part of the picture. Yang Water is said to benefit from the influence of yin Fire; this can be illustrated by the fact that an iceberg represents Water in its yang state, which needs Fire to melt it in order to make it useful.

As well as certain elements clashing with each other, elements are also said to 'combine' with each other, and this often results in another element being produced. It is on these principles that many of the astrological and feng shui calculations are based. This is one of the reasons why feng shui is such a complex subject, requiring many years of study, contemplation and experience.

Everything from acorns to zebras can be classified in terms of elements, so the chart on page 12 gives just an idea of how the elements relate to direction, colours, shapes and the seasons. Directions, colours and shapes are very important because they are used in feng shui to provide the quality of the elements that are needed for an appropriate remedy to a problem. So, if we want to introduce Wood into our lives, for example, we need to utilise the east and south-east, the colour green, shapes and designs that incorporate columns and so on.

Note that in China, the year is divided into five seasons. The Earth season occurs for the last 18 days of each of the four usual seasons, and is a time when the stabilising ch'i energy enables us to steady ourselves before the start of the next season.

ELEMENT	DIRECTION	COLOUR	SHAPES	SEASON
Wood	East and south-east	Green	Rectangles and columns	Spring
Fire	South	Red	Triangles and points	Summer
Earth	South-west and north-east	Yellow	Square and flat	Earth season
Metal	North-west and west	White	Rounded and arched	Autumn
Water	North	Black	Irregular	Winter

Positive Energy in the Home
風水

Homes and places where people live are classified as yang dwellings, while places where people are buried are classified as yin, and there is a difference between the feng shui that is applied to each one. In addition to this, feng shui can be applied in different ways depending on whether it is being used for the home or at work. In business, feng shui is often used to activate and stimulate the energy in various ways, while the purpose of feng shui in the home is to create stability, calm and harmony, and a place to replenish and rejuvenate.

If we can identify the elements and influences that occupy the various areas of the home, we then have an opportunity to try to harness these forces and get them working for us, rather than against us. If we can achieve this, we will improve our chances of 'going with the flow' and getting the maximum benefit out of the energies surrounding us.

Before using feng shui on a personal basis, it is important to look at what these influences are and how we can select which areas of our home they occupy. We can then determine how these influences affect us as individuals – and this is where the quest really begins.

Following the Emperor

In ancient China, a complete entourage of highly skilled, highly trained people was committed to ensuring that the Emperor always enjoyed good feng shui and therefore was living in harmony with the elements. For those wishing to apply basic but authentic feng shui to their home, 'following the Emperor' offers a highly auspicious path!

Fortunately for us, the value that the Chinese placed on learning and study was such that much of this ancient knowledge was written down. Although some of it has been lost, many of the writings have survived and they offer a valuable insight into how the Emperor was instructed to use feng shui in his home, the imperial palace. One of these surviving works is the ancient classic known as *Li Ch'i*, or *The Book of Rites and Ceremony*, written over 2,000 years ago. In this amazing book, these influences are not only described in detail, but their positions within the palace are clearly defined and described as the Nine Chambers of the Emperor's Palace.

The Emperor's Palace and, indeed, all important buildings in ancient China, were built with the front of the building facing south, according to the values of one of the very earliest forms of feng shui, known as Form School feng shui. This system expressed shapes, colours and contours in terms of elements and used four celestial animals to determine the four cardinal directions: the Dragon in the east, the Tiger in the west, the Tortoise in the north and the Phoenix, or Bird, in the south.

The role of the feng shui masters was both to select auspicious sites for burial – reflecting the importance of ancestor-worship to the ancient Chinese – and also to determine favourable locations for houses. As far as possible, they would select a site that resembled a horseshoe, providing the protection of hills of varying sizes on three sides, while being open at the front, facing south. Certain arrangements were considered better than others, and the ideal location was one where the hills behind the house were fairly small and rounded, like the Tortoise, and the hills on the east, or Dragon, side were larger than those on the west, or Tiger, side. The open space in the front enabled the Red Bird to fly in, and many buildings had enclosed inner courtyards and gardens into which the positive energies were channelled and contained.

In time, feng shui became more sophisticated and by the time Li Ch'i was written, calculations were in place to determine which rooms the Emperor should occupy during which season in order to live in constant harmony with the forces of Heaven and Earth. This involved extensive calculations and is the basis of what is known as the Flying Star School of feng shui.

The influence of Earth was seen in the form of the seasons, and the influence of Heaven was seen as an intangible but powerful force which determined human destiny. It was accepted that, since Heaven and Earth worked in harmony, any conflict would release negative forces.

Simple Improvements in the Home

This area of feng shui has received a lot of attention and much sound advice is already common knowledge, so since the book aims to delve a little deeper into the subject, it will not repeat information that has already been covered in so many other articles and books. This section will just give some basic tips for those who may not have come across these ideas before.

Much has been said and printed about how to use feng shui to make the most of your money. It is good feng shui to keep the toilet seat down at all times to prevent flushing money away, and it is not good to have mirrors in the bedroom – unless, of course, it is the honeymoon suite, where sleep is low on the agenda and activity is the name of the game.

Always remember that the front of the house, where the front door is situated, is regarded by the Chinese as the face of the house, which always looks better when wearing a smile. This can be easily achieved with flowers and shrubs in containers and hanging baskets, and this effect can be enhanced by selecting colours and shapes that are in harmony with the element associated with the direction the house faces.

The back of the house is equally important though, and should be kept clean and tidy at all times. Try to keep the dustbins well away from the door, and out of sight or screened off, if possible.

Keep your windows clean and replace any cracked panes immediately so that distorted ch'i cannot enter the home.

Replace broken light bulbs straight away, and install an outside light over the front door to provide what the Chinese call 'a bright hall'. Pa kua or bagua mirrors – circular mirrors surrounded by octagonal frames marked with the trigrams – should never be used in the home; they are designed to be used outside, generally over the front door, so that they may deflect any negative influences that may be directed towards the house.

Another paradox of feng shui is that, while houses for the living are described as yang dwellings, the energy inside them is considered to be yin, and only the energy outside the house considered to be yang. Because of this, houses should be made as light, airy and bright as possible, thereby fostering yang qualities that help to restore a better balance to the ch'i.

Keep clutter to a minimum. It blocks the flow of energies.

Never position chairs with their backs to a door because anyone sitting there would be vulnerable to attack from behind; in China, a guest would never be offered such a seat.

Try to avoid positioning your bed so that your feet are facing the door, since this is associated with death; remember the expression, 'taking them out feet first'.

If you like to have statues of Lord Buddha, Kuan Yin, the goddess of mercy, or other symbolic figures in the home to improve your feng shui, it would be wise to familiarise yourself with their birthdays and festivals so that you can light a candle or burn some incense in honour of the occasion. This is an a aspect of traditional feng shui that is often overlooked.

Earth Shrines

Those fortunate enough to have a garden should consider making an Earth shrine, as it is very good feng shui. It's not a religious shrine but a spiritual one, acknowledging the Earth ch'i of the garden.

An Earth shrine is easy to make and need not be large, although the more love and care that is taken, the better the result. The only important point to remember is that it must be located at ground level. It could be made of two stacks of bricks with a large flat stone or a piece of slate placed on top to act as a roof, and it should have a holder for a night light or candle inside, with anything else you like to include. The important thing is to light a candle there and leave some flowers or rose petals from time to time to acknowledge it as a special place. It provides a perfect focal point for the garden and can offer an ideal place for contemplation and meditation. Placed under a tree or in a quiet corner of the garden, these shrines are a joy to behold when illuminated with candles and decorated with flowers on festival days.

Traditional Chinese Symbols

These symbols can be used around the home – as ornaments or in pictures, for example – to engender health, wealth and happiness.

Bats
In China, the bat is considered to be a very potent symbol of good luck and happiness, not least because the Chinese word for bat sounds identical to *fu*, the word for happiness. A picture of five bats represents the five blessings: long life, wealth, happiness, virtue and a natural death.

Chinese copper coins
This is a very common symbol used extensively to generate wealth. It is said that by carrying around 'old money', you help to generate 'new money'. There is also the saying, 'Money attracts money', which is one of the reasons that money is always given to children at Chinese New Year.

Clouds
These are symbols of good fortune and happiness and they are often depicted in the five colours representing the five elements – green, white, black, red and yellow – to denote five-fold happiness. This also presents a picture of perfect harmony and, as a result, this is a potent symbol for peace.

Cranes
Although the crane is associated with longevity, it is also a potent symbol of wisdom and knowledge. A picture of two cranes flying up towards the sun is said to represent achieving a high standard in education.

Fish
Like bats, fish are also considered to be very auspicious, especially for generating wealth, and again the reason for this is that the word for fish sounds the same as *yu*, the word for abundance.

Geese
Like mandarin ducks, geese are symbols of married bliss. Chinese couples often exchange gifts decorated with the goose as engagement presents,

because the goose takes one lifelong partner, and symbols of flying geese are often used at weddings to denote getting off to a flying start.

Lilies
The Chinese believe that this wonderful flower takes away your troubles and, for that reason, they are much loved. They are also known as 'the provider of sons' and as a result they are often presented as a gift to a bride.

Lotus flowers
This is a very potent symbol of purity and to Buddhists it is one of the 'eight precious things'. In China there are two words for this flower, one that means 'unite' and one that means 'following on'.

Magnolia flowers
In China, this is commonly known as 'the flower of nocturnal togetherness'. In ancient China, only the Emperor was allowed to have magnolias, although from time to time, he would give them as gifts, denoting his pleasure.

Mandarin ducks
A common symbol for married bliss, pairs of mandarin ducks are popular symbols to place in the home.

Understanding the Portents
風水

Having given you an introduction to the most familiar elements of feng shui, we now move on to the more subtle influences at work in the home. Remember that the source of this understanding relates to the Emperor's Palace, so application of these principles relates to influencing the energies in your home.

Let us begin by looking at some of these influences that are defined in *Li Ch'i*, beginning with the heavenly ones, referred to as the portents or palaces. We can then see how to determine where they exist in our own homes.

In *Li Ch'i*, the palace is described as having nine chambers, the central one representing an open courtyard with the other eight chambers arranged round it. Each of the chambers is said to be influenced by earthly and heavenly forces. Since the palace faced south, this arrangement was seen as the benchmark, and from that calculations were made to determine where these influences were in other buildings.

It is important to stress that in *Li Ch'i*, these terms were applied to influences that occupied the chambers of the palace and therefore refer to areas within the home. You may have found these influences adapted for more popular styles of feng shui, but using these in the home is a much more authentic approach. When we combine this approach with the traditional way of determining our personal element, which we will explain in later sections, we have a system that is much closer to the original than those used by many Western consultants.

Sheng Ch'i - Source of Ch'i

This is considered by many to be the most favourable area within the home; after all, it is the source of ch'i. It is associated with a vibrant energy and as such it is an excellent area for a living room or meeting area, where family and friends gather together. An excellent location for a nursery or children's playroom, it is also ideal for those who work from home. This is an area to try to use as much as possible.

Nien Yen - Long Life

Nien yen is the perfect area for the main bedroom, especially for senior citizens who are enjoying their retirement. It is also suitable as a living room or as a workroom and is another excellent area to use, especially good for those spending a lot of time at home.

T'ien I or T'ien Yi - Heavenly Doctor

This space is the ideal location for anyone recuperating from illness of any kind – physical, emotional, spiritual or even financial – so remember, it relates to wealth as well as health. It is an excellent place to retire to when you feel a little down and need to get away from it all, or if you wish to meditate. It is also very favourable for t'ai ch'i, aerobics or other forms of exercise.

Fu Wei - Bowing to the Throne

This is always located at the entrance of the home because, upon entering the palace, you would be expected to bow to the throne. That being the case, this area is also considered to be auspicious, since not everyone is fortunate enough to have access to the palace and those who do are favoured.

Wu Kuei - Five Ghosts

In traditional Chinese homes, the family shrine is often located in this area, where candles are lit and incense is burnt as offerings to their ancestors, as well as all the occupants of Heaven. If you have statues of Buddha, Kuan Yin or other symbolic characters, this would be a good place to keep them in order to obtain their help in eliminating the negative effects of hungry ghosts and bad spirits.

Liu Sha - Six Curses or Six Imps

This area relates to minor annoying mishaps that keep recurring - the Western saying is that accidents happen in threes, but in China they say that they are repeated six times. This is therefore an area to watch, because if you find that something goes wrong here, the chances are that it will be repeated. If you find yourself arguing with your partner or shouting at the children here, try to avoid spending too much time in this area; if you find yourself having accidents here, exercise more caution than usual.

Hai Huo - Accidents and Mishaps

As the name suggests, this is an accident-prone area and is therefore not very suitable for a child's bedroom or playroom. If this cannot be avoided, then do take extra care. This applies equally to adults, especially if the kitchen is situated in this area of the house, in which case everyone should be particularly careful when using sharp knives or cooking.

Chueh Ming - Broken or Severed Fate

Although the most unfavourable area of the home, this should not be viewed as a no-go area. Not only will it affect different people in different ways, but its influence changes from year to year and month to month according to the Flying Stars (see pages 27–32). It is important to stress this because if you cannot avoid having your bedroom in this area, for example, don't assume everything is doom and gloom. Calculate your personal element using the system on pages 57–60, then read the appropriate section on the best action to take.

Using the Portents

These are the energies that are influential in the main areas of your home and these calculations form the basis of what are known as the eight mansions, or houses. By identifying the direction your front door faces, and using the following charts, you will be able to determine where these influences appear in your home.

These authentic principles offer everyone the chance to utilise the same advice that was given to the Emperor. Understanding where these portents are located, depending on the direction of the main door, is essential before you can progress to anything more complex. Later in the book, we will look at the refinement of the eight mansions, in which each mansion is sub-divided into three units, giving the 24 mountain stars (see pages 33–8). This is known as Flying Star feng shui.

The following charts show the position of the energies in the house, as defined in the previous chapter, depending on the direction in which the main door faces.

Each chart is set out according to the direction of the main door, so in the chart for a house facing north, the main door is facing north, and in the chart for a house facing south-west, the main door is facing south-west, and so on.

HOUSE FACING SOUTH		
Chueh ming Broken fate	Nien yen Long life	Hai huo Accidents
Wu kuei Five ghosts		Sheng ch'i Source of ch'i
Liu sha Six curses	Fu wei Bowing to the throne ↓ South	T'ien I Heavenly doctor

HOUSE FACING SOUTH-WEST		
Chueh ming Broken fate	Sheng ch'i Source of ch'i	Hai huo Accidents
Nien yen Long life		Wu kuei Five ghosts
T'ien I Heavenly doctor	Fu wei Bowing to the throne ↓ South-west	Liu sha Six curses

HOUSE FACING WEST		
Nien yen Long life	Chueh ming Broken fate	Liu sha Six curses
Hai huo Accidents		Wu kuei Five ghosts
Sheng ch'i Source of ch'i	Fu wei Bowing to the throne ↓ West	T'ien I Heavenly doctor

HOUSE FACING NORTH-WEST		
Wu kuei Five ghosts	Hai huo Accidents	Chueh ming Broken fate
T'ien I Heavenly doctor		Nien yen Long life
Liu sha Six curses	Fu wei Bowing to the throne ↓ North-west	Sheng ch'i Source of ch'i

HOUSE FACING NORTH		
Sheng ch'i Source of ch'i	*Nien yen* Long life	*Chueh ming* Broken fate
T'ien I Heavenly doctor		*Hai huo* Accidents
Wu kuei Five ghosts	*Fu wei* Bowing to the throne ↓ North	*Liu sha* Six curses

HOUSE FACING NORTH-EAST		
Hai huo Accidents	*Sheng ch'i* Source of ch'i	*Nien yen* Long life
Chueh ming Broken fate		*T'ien I* Heavenly doctor
Liu sha Six curses	*Fu wei* Bowing to the throne ↓ North-east	*Wu kuei* Five ghosts

HOUSE FACING EAST		
Hai huo Accidents	*Chueh ming* Broken fate	*Wu kuei* Five ghosts
Sheng ch'i Source of ch'i		*T'ien I* Heavenly doctor
Nien yen Long life	*Fu wei* Bowing to the throne ↓ East	*Liu sha* Six curses

HOUSE FACING SOUTH-EAST		
Liu sha Six curses	*Hai huo* Accidents	*Sheng ch'i* Source of ch'i
Wu kuei Five ghosts		*Chueh ming* Broken fate
T'ien I Heavenly doctor	*Fu wei* Bowing to the throne	*Nien yen* Long life
	↓ South-east	

Find the relevant chart for your house direction, then by imposing the plan of the Emperor's Palace over your own floor plan, you can see which energies relate to the different areas of your home. If you can reorganise the use of your rooms to maximise the energies, that could be advantageous.

The Directions and the Elements

風水

ach of the eight compass directions can be associated with one of the five elements. Each area in a house is therefore associated with an element, and each house is associated with the element that relates to the direction in which the front door faces.

The eight directions are linked with the five elements in two ways, known as the Former Heaven Sequence and the Later Heaven Sequence. The latter is also known as the Magic Square, because each element and direction is also related to a number, and the positions of the numbers in the square are such that the lines add up to 15 in all directions.

4	9	2
3	5	7
8	1	6

It is this arrangement that many feng shui masters use and, for our purposes, we will apply it to determine the element for each direction. From this and the table below we can see that a north-facing house – which relates to the number one – relates to Water, a house facing south-west relates to Earth, and so on.

Wood South- east	Fire South	Earth South- west
Wood East		Metal West
Earth North- east	Water North	Metal North- west

If we compare the house element with the element associated with each area, an interesting picture begins to emerge. Let's consider some examples. If you look at the portents for a north-facing house (see page 22), which represents Water, the portent *chueh ming* is in the south-west, an area associated with the Earth element. Since Earth is said to control or destroy Water, it is not surprising that this area is said to be in conflict; and as a result, negative ch'i is created.

In a house facing east (see page 22), associated with Wood, *chueh ming* is located in the west, which is associated with Metal. Since Metal is said to control Wood, this is another area in conflict.

In a house facing north-west (see page 21), associated with Metal, *chueh ming* is in the south, associated with Fire, and since Fire is said to destroy Metal, this area is again in conflict.

In contrast, in a house facing south-east (see page 23), associated with Wood, the area associated with *sheng ch'i*, the source of ch'i, is located in the north, which is associated with Water. Since Water and Wood are in harmony, this area is considered to be in harmony.

In a house facing south-west (see page 21), associated with Earth, *sheng ch'i* is located in the north-east, which is also associated with the Earth element, so once again there does not appear to be any conflict.

The solution to such conflicts is to refer back to the cycles of generation of the elements and add representations of supportive elements with a view to restoring the balance of elemental energies. For example, where Metal and Fire are in conflict, you could add Earth to support the Metal or Water to dowse the Fire.

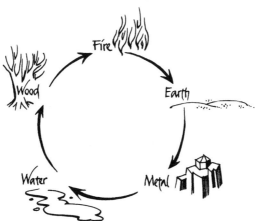

Odd-shaped Houses

It is important to remember that these calculations are based on the Emperor's Palace, a house with the door in the middle and a central courtyard, not necessarily the pattern for most modern houses. This may cause confusion, because some areas of the house are often described as 'missing', but we can make adjustments accordingly.

The entrance is always associated with the *fu wei* energies so, if the door is located on the right-hand side as you face it, the usual portents associated with that area could be said to be missing. The same is true if the door is to the left. Long, narrow houses can also be regarded as having missing areas, as you would 'lose' the portents at the top, and if the door is also on one side, you would lose other areas as well. If you are a student living in one room, then in theory you only have *fu wei* energies, which are always favourable.

In these cases, each room can be divided into energy areas in the same way as the house itself. In this case of a single room, for example, you should therefore site your bed in one of the favourable areas, determined by the direction of the door.

Introducing the Flying Stars
風水

As we said earlier, Flying Star feng shui is a development of the use of the eight portents, and the application of these principles is favoured by the vast majority of the traditional Chinese masters, who use it to determine how good, and bad, fortune is likely to affect a home. Understanding these principles, rather than simply those of the portents, allows you to be more precise in your knowledge and application of Chinese principles in order to make improvements in the energies in your home.

There are nine stars in all and they are identified by a specific number and colour. The nine numbers can be represented in what is often called the Magic Square or *lo shu:* a square in which all the numbers add up to 15 in any direction. The name 'flying stars' is derived from the fact that they move in a predetermined pattern around the square. The most common arrangement of the stars is defined as the Later Heaven arrangement.

South-east 4 Green	South 9 Purple	South-west 2 Black
East 3 Green	Centre 5 Yellow	West 7 Red
North-east 8 White	North 1 White	North-west 6 White

The Birth Chart for a House

We have already seen that the energies flowing through a house are influenced by the direction in which the main door faces. In addition to this, the age, or what is often referred to as the period of a building, is a crucial factor, as this is used to create what is often called the birth chart for the house. Houses, like people, have periods of good and bad luck and this system enables us to get a basic guide to how the positive and negative fortunes associated with a specific house are likely to fluctuate with time.

Time is expressed in cycles of 180 years, each known as a *yuan*. Each yuan is subdivided into nine cycles of 20 years, with each cycle represented by one of the nine flying stars. Each 20-year cycle will therefore have a different ruling star, and after 180 years, the cycle begins again. Each new yuan begins with the number 1 star as the ruling star and ends with the number 9 star, so the cycle follows a yang progression, which means the cycles move forward through the numbers. The current 180-year cycle began in 1864, so the period 1984–2003 is governed by the number 7 star. A new period begins in 2004, when the number 8 star will become the ruling star.

The age of a building, in feng shui terms, is defined by the 20-year period in which it was built, so a house built in 2000 would be regarded as a number 7 or period 7 house, because it was built when 7 was the ruling star of the period. You can usually find the construction date for your property from the house deeds or local land registers. You can then see from the table below the ruling star period for your home.

YEARS	NUMBER	COLOUR
1864–1883	1	White
1884–1903	2	Black
1904–1923	3	Green
1924–1943	4	Green
1944–1963	5	Yellow
1964–1983	6	White
1984–2003	7	Red
2004–2023	8	White
2024–2043	9	Purple

As we have said, the stars move around the chart in a predetermined pattern, so they will appear in a specific direction, depending on the ruling star. For each of the cycles, the ruling star is placed in the centre of the magic square, while the remaining stars are positioned in numerical sequence in a set pattern around the square. The Later Heaven arrangement, with yellow 5 in the centre, establishes the flight path for the flying stars. The numbers move from north to south-west, to east, to south-east, to centre, to north-west, to west, to north-east, to south.

To construct a birth chart for your house, refer to the relevant chart on the next pages.

PERIOD 1 HOUSE		
South-east Number 9 Purple	South Number 5 Yellow	South-west Number 7 Red
East Number 8 White	Centre Number 1 White	West Number 3 Green
North-east Number 4 Green	North Number 6 White	North-west Number 2 Black

PERIOD 2 HOUSE		
South-east Number 1 White	South Number 6 White	South-west Number 8 White
East Number 9 Purple	Centre Number 2 Black	West Number 4 Green
North-east Number 5 Yellow	North Number 7 Red	North-west Number 3 Green

PERIOD 3 HOUSE		
South-east Number 2 Black	South Number 7 Red	South-west Number 9 Purple
East Number 1 White	Centre Number 3 Green	West Number 5 Yellow
North-east Number 6 White	North Number 8 White	North-west Number 4 Green

PERIOD 4 HOUSE		
South-east Number 3 Green	South Number 8 White	South-west Number 1 White
East Number 2 Black	Centre Number 4 Green	West Number 6 White
North-east Number 7 Red	North Number 9 Purple	North-west Number 5 Yellow

PERIOD 5 HOUSE		
South-east Number 4 Green	South Number 9 Purple	South-west Number 2 Black
East Number 3 Green	Centre Number 5 Yellow	West Number 7 Red
North-east Number 8 White	North Number 1 White	North-west Number 6 White

PERIOD 6 HOUSE		
South-east Number 5 Yellow	South Number 1 White	South-west Number 3 Green
East Number 4 Green	Centre Number 6 White	West Number 8 White
North-east Number 9 Purple	North Number 2 Black	North-west Number 7 Red

PERIOD 7 HOUSE		
South-east Number 6 White	South Number 2 Black	South-west Number 4 Green
East Number 5 Yellow	Centre Number 7 Red	West Number 9 Purple
North-east Number 1 White	North Number 3 Green	North-west Number 8 White

PERIOD 8 HOUSE		
South-east Number 7 Red	South Number 3 Green	South-west Number 5 Yellow
East Number 6 White	Centre Number 8 White	West Number 1 White
North-east Number 2 Black	North Number 4 Green	North-west Number 9 Purple

PERIOD 9 HOUSE		
South-east Number 8 White	South Number 4 Green	South-west Number 6 White
East Number 7 Red	Centre Number 9 Purple	West Number 2 Black
North-east Number 3 Green	North Number 5 Yellow	North-west Number 1 White

Your Lucky Stars

In general terms, some stars are considered to be lucky and others not, and the following table serves as a guide to the lucky associations of each of the stars.

NUMBER	COLOUR	LUCK
Number 1	White	Lucky
Number 2	Black	Unlucky
Number 3	Green	Variable
Number 4	Green	Lucky
Number 5	Yellow	Unlucky
Number 6	White	Lucky
Number 7	Red	Variable
Number 8	White	Lucky
Number 9	Purple	Variable

Using the Lucky Stars

As with much of feng shui, the importance of this lies in the combinations of energies. You have already established the strength and quality of the various energies that relate to the different areas of your home, as determined by the direction of the main door. Now that you have constructed a birth chart for your house, you have established the lucky and unlucky areas of the home that relate to the year in which the property was built. We shall next examine how these interact with each other. The best possible option is that the area influenced by *sheng ch'i* also falls under a lucky star, in which case this should be the area of your home you use the most as this will offer the most favourable aspects. If negative aspects combine, then you need to make every effort to minimise the importance of the activities that take place in that part of the home.

More About the Flying Stars

風水

The next logical development of the Flying Stars is to subdivide the eight portents into the 24 directions. These directions are usually known as the 24 Mountain Stars and they are used to identify the star that is associated both with the front and the back of the building. This gives an increased subtlety to the interpretation of your home. This book can only offer a basic guide to the Flying Stars, as to master the complexities of the system really takes considerable study. However, it should give you a better understanding of how the system works and how to make simple applications.

The front of the house is known as the facing direction, the Facing or Water Star, while the back is known as the sitting direction, the Sitting or Mountain Star. Using a compass and the chart below, you can determine these stars for your house.

You will see from the chart on page 34 that each of the 24 directions relates to 15 degrees of the compass. Once we reach this level of sophistication, you therefore need to know the exact direction in which your house faces, rather than just the approximate direction. North is the mid-point of the Rat direction, east is the mid-point of the Rabbit direction, south is the mid-point of the Horse direction and west is the mid-point of the Rooster direction.

Another important aspect to note is that the directions are also associated with yin and yang. In this instance, yang relates to a forward progression and yin relates to a backwards progression, and this is used to calculate how the stars fly around the house. Some fly in a forward numerical order while others fly backwards, and this forms the basis of all calculations. The directions are measured from the north.

MOUNTAIN STAR	COMPASS DIRECTION	ACCURATE DIRECTION
Horse *Wu* (yin)	South	172.5°–187.5°
Yin Fire *Ding* (yin)	South	187.5°–202.5°
Sheep *Wei* (yin)	South-west	202.5°–217.5°
Earth *Kun* (yang)	South-west	217.5°–232.5°
Monkey *Shen* (yang)	South-west	232.5°–247.5°
Yang Metal *Geng* (yang)	West	247.5°–262.5°
Rooster *Yu* (yin)	West	262.5°–277.5°
Yin Metal *Xin* (yin)	West	277.5°–292.5°
Dog *Xu* (yin)	North-west	292.5°–307.5°
Heaven *Qian* (yang)	North-west	307.5°–322.5°
Pig *Hai* (yang)	North-west	322.5°–337.5°
Yang Water *Ren* (yang)	North	337.5°–352.5°
Rat *Zi* (yin)	North	352.5°–7.5°
Yin Water *Gui* (yin)	North	7.5°–022.5°
Ox *Chu* (yin)	North-east	22.5°–37.5°
Mountain *Gen* (yang)	North-east	37.5°–52.5°
Tiger *Yin* (yang)	North-east	52.5°–67.5°
Yang Wood *Jia* (yang)	East	67.5°–82.5°
Rabbit *Mao* (yin)	East	82.5°–97.5°
Yin Wood *Yi* (yin)	East	97.5°–112.5°
Dragon *Chen* (yin)	South-east	112.5°–127.5°
Wind *Xun* (yang)	South-east	127.5°–142.5°
Snake *Si* (yang)	South-east	142.5°–157.5°
Yang Fire *Bing* (yang)	South	157.5°–172.5°

The Flight Path of the Mountain Stars

The Mountain Stars move through the compass directions in the same way as the period stars, circulating in a predetermined pattern around the ruling star in the centre. The only difference is that some stars move forwards, and others backwards. Now let us look at a specific example:

South-east 3 Green	South 8 White	South-west 1 White
East 2 Black	Centre 4 Green	West 6 White
North-east 7 Red	North 9 Purple	North-west 5 Yellow

The example on page 34 uses a house built in 1926. By examining the information in this table, we can see that this is a number 4 house.

The next thing to establish is the direction in which the house faces to determine the Facing or Water Star. Let us say that we know the house faces roughly east, but a compass reading defines this specifically as 80 degrees. By referring to the chart at the top of page 34, we can see that this is part of the Mountain Star called Yang Wood and it is yang. Since this Mountain Star is in the east, we use the star in the east from the example at the bottom of page 34: number 2 Black. This becomes the Facing Star for our example house and is placed in the centre. Since it is yang, it moves forwards in numerical order, using the same flight path as the Earth chart.

South-east	South	South-west
Facing Star: I	**Facing Star: 6**	**Facing Star: 8**
White	**White**	**White**
Period Star: 3	**Period Star: 8**	**Period Star: I**
Green	**White**	**White**
East	**Centre**	**West**
Facing Star: 9	**Facing Star: 2**	**Facing Star: 4**
Purple	**Black**	**Green**
Period Star: 2	**Period Star: 4**	**Period Star: 6**
Black	**Green**	**White**
North-east	**North**	**North-west**
Facing Star: 5	**Facing Star: 7**	**Facing Star: 3**
Yellow	**Red**	**Green**
Period Star: 7	**Period Star: 9**	**Period Star: 5**
Red	**Purple**	**Yellow**

The next step is to determine the Sitting or Mountain Star, which relates to the direction that the back of the house faces. If the front faces East, then the back will face the West and using a compass, we discover that it faces 260 degrees. Looking once again at the conversion chart on page 34, we can see that this relates to the Mountain Star called Yang Metal, which is also yang.

Since this Mountain Star belongs to the west, the Earth chart confirms that the Period Star in the west is Number 6 White. This becomes the Mountain Star for this house and is placed in the centre, in the same way that we placed the Water Star. Since it is also yang, it also flies forwards in numerical order, using the same flight path as the Earth chart.

The final chart on page 36 represents a typical Flying Star chart, with each area represented by three stars: the Period Star, the Mountain Star and the Water Star.

South-east **Facing Star: 1** **White** **Period Star: 3** **Green** **Mountain Star: 5** **Yellow**	**South** **Facing Star: 6** **White** **Period Star: 8** **White** **Mountain Star: 1** **White**	**South-west** **Facing Star: 8** **White** **Period Star: 1** **White** **Mountain Star: 3** **Green**
East **Facing Star: 9** **Purple** **Period Star: 2** **Black** **Mountain Star: 4** **Green**	**Centre** **Facing Star: 2** **Black** **Period Star: 4** **Green** **Mountain Star: 6** **White**	**West** **Facing Star: 4** **Green** **Period Star: 6** **White** **Mountain Star: 8** **White**
North-east **Facing Star: 5** **Yellow** **Period Star: 7** **Red** **Mountain Star: 9** **Purple**	**North** **Facing Star: 7** **Red** **Period Star: 9** **Purple** **Mountain Star: 2** **Black**	**North-west** **Facing Star: 3** **Green** **Period Star: 5** **Yellow** **Mountain Star: 7** **Red**

The Period Stars and the Ruling Star

Feng shui is dynamic and is therefore constantly changing. No building will always be in a period of good luck; it will change from being in a lucky period to a changeable to an unlucky one. Therefore, if your home or office is defined as being in a favourable period, you must make the most of those positive energies while they are in operation. On the other hand, if your building is in an unfavourable period, you can minimise the negative influences, as described in this book, and be reassured that your luck is certain to improve in time.

One simple way of looking at this is to use the Period Star of the building – referring to the tables on pages 29–31 – and compare this with the Ruling Stars for the present period.

The fortunes of a building change with each 20-year period, as explained on page 28. Some periods bring great prosperity, while others signify a decline in good fortune. The following tables provide a basic guide to how the fortunes of buildings with different Period Stars will be affected by the overall Ruling Stars. It shows a general trend for all buildings in all years. For example, if your house was built in 1940, it will be a period 4 house. The year 2002 is in period 7, so the Ruling Stars for that year is 7. Since 7 is a neutral stage for a period 4 house, the fortunes of that property should be relatively even during that period. When the Ruling Stars changes in 2004 and we enter period 8, the fortunes of the house should improve. The tables highlight the most positive energies. Remember that you can still make sensible and positive use of all energies.

BUILDING	PERIOD 1	PERIOD 2	PERIOD 3	PERIOD 4
Period 1	Good		Good	Good
Period 2	Good	Good		
Period 3	Neutral	Good	Good	
Period 4	Good	Good	Good	Good
Period 5				Good
Period 6	Good	Good	Good	Good
Period 7		Neutral	Good	
Period 8	Good	Good	Good	Good
Period 9				Neutral

BUILDING	PERIOD 5	PERIOD 6	PERIOD 7	PERIOD 8	PERIOD 9
Period 1	Good	Good	Good	Good	Good
Period 2			Neutral	Good	
Period 3				Good	
Period 4		Good	Neutral	Good	Good
Period 5	Good				
Period 6	Good	Good		Good	Good
Period 7		Good	Good		
Period 8	Good	Good	Good	Good	
Period 9			Neutral	Good	Good

There are many factors that determine how the energies in these tables are defined and it is beyond the scope of this book to explain the reasons behind those definitions. However, it is interesting to focus on certain aspects.

The first thing to notice is that some buildings enjoy more good fortune than others, depending on the period in which they were built. Houses built in Periods 1, 6 and 8 enjoy more favourable periods than others, while those built during periods 2 and 5 enjoy the least. It is no coincidence that 1, 6 and 8 are considered to be Lucky Stars, while 2 and 5 are considered unlucky. Another significant point is that a house always enjoys good fortune during the period in which it was built, so a period 3 house always has good fortune during period 3, a period 7 house is always considered to be favourable during period 7, and so on.

The Flying Stars and the Elements

Each of the flying stars is also associated with an element and this provides another avenue to explore when looking at the various combinations.

FLYING STAR	ELEMENT	FLYING STAR	ELEMENT
1 White	Water	6 White	Metal
2 Black	Earth	7 Red	Metal
3 Green	Wood	8 White	Earth
4 Green	Wood	9 Purple	Fire
5 Yellow	Earth		

Feng shui is all about harmony and balance and encouraging the beneficial flow of ch'i, and the five elements play a crucial role. In an ideal world, all five elements are present in a balanced proportion, but where there is conflict, additional elements need to be introduced to restore that balance. In our period 4 house with a facing direction of 80 degrees, we can add the relevant elements to the table of all the stars.

South-east	South	South-west
Facing Star: 1	Facing Star: 6	Facing Star: 8
White Water	White Metal	White Earth
Period Star: 3	Period Star: 8	Period Star: 1
Green Wood	White Earth	White Water
Mountain Star: 5	Mountain Star: 1	Mountain Star: 3
Yellow Earth	White Water	Green Wood
East	**Centre**	**West**
Facing Star: 9	Facing Star: 2	Facing Star: 4
Purple Fire	Black Earth	Green Wood
Period Star: 2	Period Star: 4	Period Star: 6
Black Earth	Green Wood	White Metal
Mountain Star: 4	Mountain Star: 6	Mountain Star: 8
Green Wood	White Metal	White Earth
North-east	**North**	**North-west**
Facing Star: 5	Facing Star: 7	Facing Star: 3
Yellow Earth	Red Metal	Green Wood
Period Star: 7	Period Star: 9	Period Star: 5
Red Metal	Purple Fire	Yellow Earth
Mountain Star: 9	Mountain Star: 2	Mountain Star: 7
Purple Fire	Black Earth	Red Metal

The chart shows that some of the combinations are in harmony while others are not. In the area associated with the south, the combination of 6, 8 and 1 is represented by Earth, Metal and Water. Since Earth generates Metal, which generates Water, this combination is in harmony. The area associated with the North is also in harmony, being represented by 7, 9 and 2, Fire, Earth and Metal.

The area associated with the North-west is not so fortunate, because the elements are Earth, Metal and Wood. Earth generates Metal but attacks Wood, so it would be advisable to add Water to restore harmony and balance. The Earth could then generate Metal, which would generate Water, which in turn would generate Wood. The addition of the Water element would provide the Metal with a positive outlet so instead of attacking Wood, it would generate Water, which would then generate Wood and restore harmony.

Positive Energy at Work
風水

We are now going to move away from the home and discover how the Chinese view the Earth energies affecting them at work. Since your home and your workplace represent different parts of your life, it makes sense that they respond to different energies. The home is a place for stability, where you have time to relax, to spend time with your family and enjoy the company of friends. Although everyone likes a degree of spontaneous energy at home, an over-active, over-crowded house where everyone is coming and going all the time does not create the ideal living space. When you apply feng shui to your home, it is with the intention of harmonising your living space with stable energies. Business feng shui, on the other hand, is designed to activate and stimulate change, to make things happen. A quiet, tranquil, peaceful shop, for example, is not conducive to good business.

Although, as we have said, there are a number of different styles of feng shui, some consultants tend to treat an assessment of a business in the same way that they approach an assessment of a home, but this is not always the most effective approach. When we look at the home, we relate each area of the house to the areas of the Emperor's Palace and align the energies in the most auspicious directions. This is because feng shui was originally devised to help the Emperor live in harmony with the elements and the energies surrounding him and we try to emulate the same benefits today. However, since activating and stimulating change is the objective of business feng shui, the emphasis should be on these aspects of the premises and not on the same influences that affect our lives at home. Therefore, while feng shui at home harnesses the energies relating to harmony, long life and stability, feng shui in business focuses on energies associated with change and transformation.

Good Practice at Work

It is important to remember that although buildings where people live and work are considered to be yang dwellings, the energy contained inside them is considered to be yin; therefore if your business, workplace or shop has a security system at the door, where any potential customer has to ring a bell, this will enhance the yin aspect even more, since anything closed is associated with yin, whereas anything open is associated with yang. Balance and harmony are the crucial factors and a brightly illuminated bell would help to introduce the yang aspect, which would then restore the balance and encourage customers or clients to come to the business, while still paying attention to the security aspects. If you have an illuminated door bell, it is important to check that the bulb is always working, since if the light goes out it denotes that you are not open for business.

The nature of yang is light, bright and spacious and these aspects should be harnessed in order to activate and stimulate the energy within the business. Shops benefit particularly from being light and spaciously designed as this actively encourages people to enter and move around. Lighting is particularly important in all businesses, since this introduces the yang aspect, helping to activate and generate the positive ch'i within the premises.

Shop window displays also benefit from being brightly lit and attractive in order to stimulate and inspire those who pass by, but they should also be in harmony with the element of the business, as well as the element influencing the direction that the window faces. Seasonal variations should also be taken into account, because the most positive energies are harnessed if the window display works in harmony with the element of the season. New Year decorations, for example, are very bright and positive, reminding us of the new, active energy to come.

As in all feng shui considerations, avoid rubbish and clutter and keep offices, factories or any other business premises tidy. Keep premises clean, too, and make sure that windows are clean and sparkling so that they allow the maximum positive energies to enter the building. This is especially true in offices where people need to be inspired and motivated. Attractive furniture and office equipment, good lighting, paintings and plants can all be used to bring favourable influences into the office.

To be in command of your space, position yourself where you can see the door so that you will never be caught unawares. If you work in an open-plan office, try to ensure that the desks and screens are carefully placed so that people are not working with their backs to the door, or facing blank walls or panels.

If you work from home, try to make sure your office room is separate from your living space, so that you can encourage the relevant energies surrounding those aspects of your life. If it is not possible to have a room designated as your office, try not to place your desk or office space in your bedroom or the place where you like to relax. If you can screen the work place off from the rest of the room, that can sometimes be helpful.

Choosing the Right Time

Moving into new premises should always be carried out on an auspicious day. Although many will view this as an astrological aspect, the Chinese way of determining such matters is also closely related to metaphysics. Many traditional Chinese doctors take into consideration not only the best treatment, but also the best time to treat their patients, relating time in terms of elements and using those that are in harmony with the treatment.

The *T'ung Shu Almanac*, one of the most widely distributed books in China, is generally consulted in matters of business, not only to decide if it is a good day to move into new premises but also to select appropriate dates for meetings, signing of contracts and even appropriate times for investment. The Western mind may well smile at this approach, but to the Chinese, this is perfectly natural because this allows them to 'go with the flow', harnessing the power of positive energies and diminishing the influence of negative ones.

Luck is considered an important issue to the Chinese, especially when it comes to matters relating to business, and the Chinese believe everyone should make the most of the good luck that comes their way. This is one of the reasons why most traditional Chinese feng shui masters use their clients' dates of birth to determine what 'fate cycles' they are in, or what elements are influencing them at any given time.

In Chinese terms, this is very important because it is said that in a good fate period we tend to make good decisions, but in a bad fate period our judgment is often not at its best. There is much more on this aspect of the study of fate cycles on pages 149–55.

Introducing the
Eight Trigrams

風水

The one area of common ground that binds all the schools of feng shui is the use of trigrams. Since the trigrams form such an integral part of the subject, it is important to have an understanding of the major principles involved in order to see what the trigrams represent and how they work.

Like the principles of yin and yang and the theory of the five elements, knowledge and use of trigrams can be traced back thousands of years. Fortunately, a great deal of information about trigrams has survived the centuries in the form of the *I Ching*, or *Yi Jing*, known as *The Book of Changes*. It is one of the oldest surviving ancient Chinese classics and is devoted entirely to a study of the trigrams.

Each trigram consists of three lines. The lines are defined as either yin or yang: complete, uninterrupted lines are considered to be yang, while broken lines are considered to be yin. The top line of each trigram represents Heaven, the bottom line Earth, and the middle line, humans, existing between the two. This concept encapsulates what feng shui is all about: the study of the forces of Heaven and Earth and how we interact with them.

Rather than looking at the trigrams individually, *I Ching* places them in pairs, one on top of the other, to produce an upper and lower trigram. Since there are eight trigrams in all, this results in 64 possible combinations. In *I Ching*, they are referred to as the 64 hexagrams, as they each have six lines rather than three.

The fusion of the two trigrams creates a transformation, or type of change, which is associated with the hexagram. In China, they use this transformation to provide the basis for interpretation and therefore *I Ching* is usually regarded as a book of fortune-telling. If someone has a specific question to which they are seeking an answer, they select a hexagram using various systems involving throwing coins or yarrow stalks. The chosen hexagram provides the answer to their question.

Each of the eight trigrams is associated with one of the five elements as well as being defined as either yin or yang. Most importantly, each one is associated with a different type of change.

Ch'ien: Heaven, The Creative, The Father, Yang Metal

Ch'ien represents the yang principle at its peak, signified by three yang lines. The Chinese character for *ch'ien* can be broken down into various parts, which can be interpreted as meaning 'the first perfect day'. This is why this trigram relates to Heaven, even though the Chinese character for Heaven is quite different.

Ch'ien is said to encourage inspiration, creativity and spontaneity and these characteristics provide the ideal location for jobs which demand this type of atmosphere and skill. In an office or factory, this would indicate the ideal area to locate the design or marketing departments or the offices of those controlling the business, so that the people who work with ideas and who are seeking inspiration can make the best use of the surrounding energies. In a shop, this would be a good area to place items which you want to draw to the attention of potential customers, especially items which are generally purchased on impulse.

K'un: Earth, The Receptive, The Mother, Yin Earth

K'un represents the yin principle at its peak, signified by three yin lines. The Chinese character for *k'un* contains the character for Earth combined with a character that can be translated as 'compliant'. The combination of these characters gives the interpretation 'complying with Mother Earth'.

K'un is said to represent natural change: the way that plants, humans and other animals grow and the seasons flow into each other. It is a stable and passive energy, moving forward slowly and rhythmically. In an office or factory, this would indicate an ideal location for the staff canteen, since this trigram is also associated with nourishment, but it would also be a good place to position a nursery or laboratory, or anywhere where things grow or are nurtured. In a shop, this area could be used for items that are sold regularly but which are updated, especially those that are seasonal.

Chen: Thunder, To Arouse, The Eldest Son, Yang Wood

Chen represents the yang principle at an early stage, pushing upwards, signified by a yang line at the bottom with two yin lines above it. The Chinese character for *chen* also contains the character for rain, which of course often follows thunder, as well as another character which is associated with the Dragon of Spring. This denotes the arousal of activity as a positive response to the complacency and inertia of the winter period.

Chen is associated with a change of place, with linear movement and things moving from one place to the next. In a factory or office, this would be the ideal area to place the despatch department, where goods are collected ready to be sent out from the building. In a shop, this area could be used for items waiting to be delivered, or for goods that are purchased for holidays or travel. It is also a good area to place items that have been reduced in price so that they can be sold quickly to make room for new stock.

K'an: The Abyss, Water, The Middle Son, Yang Water

K'an represents the yang principle under attack from yin, signified by a yang line in the centre surrounded by two yin lines. The Chinese character for k'an consists of the character for Earth, coupled with a character which represents a hole or an empty pit. By combining these two, we can see where the idea of the abyss comes from, as well as the element of danger.

K'an is associated with rotational change, best symbolised by the water wheel. In a factory, this would be the ideal area to place machinery that runs continuously or applications that use a conveyor belt. In an office, it would be appropriate for any task that happens all the time. In a shop, this area would be ideal to place rotating or revolving display units or for goods which are constantly changing, like new lines or the latest fashions.

Ken: The Mountain, Keeping Still, The Youngest Son, Yang Earth

Ken represents the yang principle at its weakest, signified by a yang line at the top being pushed out by the two yin lines underneath, which are rising upwards. The Chinese character for ken can be translated as 'obstinate' or 'resistant', possibly denoting the unwillingness of the single yang line to submit to the yin pressure.

Ken represents unchanging, constant and stable energies and in a factory or office this would indicate an ideal place for storage of goods, company records or even money in the safe. It is also an ideal location for the office of anyone in charge of security. In a shop, this would be the place to site the cash register or any goods which need to be kept secure.

Sun: The Wind, Penetrating, The Eldest Daughter, Yin Wood

Sun represents the yin principle pushing upwards, signified by a yin line at the bottom with two yang lines above it. The Chinese character for sun consists of a double image of the character that represents a seal or stamp, emphasising a binding agreement, with a character which translates as 'following on'. This presents an image of binding contracts that apply to both relationships and business affairs.

Sun represents continuity as well as a change of form, which is best symbolised by the process of turning a piece of wood into a table. This is the perfect area to carry out routine and methodical tasks that often go unnoticed but which are fundamental for good business. This area is also associated with trading and is therefore a good location for those who are looking for new outlets for the business. In a shop, this is a good location for advertising and promotions.

Li: Radiance, Illuminating, The Middle Daughter, Yin Fire

Li represents the yin principle under attack from yang, signified by a yin line in the centre surrounded by two yang lines. The Chinese character for *li* is the most complicated of all the characters representing the trigrams. One of the characters that make up the character for li relates to a short-tailed, bright bird, similar to the phoenix, but there is also a reference to a malignant force. The overall impression is that the brightness radiates and spreads out, thus overcoming the negative aspects.

Li represents a change of substance or chemical change as well as anything to do with heat. This makes it an ideal location for the furnaces in a foundry, the ovens in a bakery or major heating installations. In a shop, this would be an ideal location for things that are bright and radiant, as well as stock associated with vision or intellect.

Tui: The Lake, Joy, The Youngest Daughter, Yin Metal

Tui represents the yin principle in its most vulnerable state, signified by the yin line at the top being pushed out by the two yang lines underneath, both pushing upwards. The Chinese character for *tui* consists of characters that relate to pleasure and also barter and exchange, denoting joy and happiness that is shared and exchanged.

Tui is said to be associated with psychological change and although it is associated with pleasure and joy, it is also reflective. Anything to do with entertainment and recreation would be ideally placed in this area, but processes involving delicate precision are also well favoured. In a shop, this is an ideal area to use for goods that are joyful and happy as well as pretty and delicate.

The Arrangements of the Trigrams

風水

The element and type of change associated with each trigram remains constant, but the direction associated with each one changes, depending on which arrangement of the symbols is used. The two most commonly used arrangements are the Former Heaven Sequence and the Later Heaven Sequence which we have already looked at on page 27 in relation to the Flying Stars.

This aspect of feng shui has caused some confusion because the Chinese themselves have been deliberating for thousands of years to determine the reason for this change in arrangements; some styles of feng shui refer to the Former Heaven arrangement while others favour the Later Heaven arrangement.

One theory is that since the Chinese people themselves migrated to China from the west, they needed to realign the arrangement in keeping with their new home. Another theory is that the Former Heaven arrangement represents a time when the world was at peace, but when wars and conflict began, a new arrangement was needed. The Taoist view is that Former Heaven represents the world in its creative state, before the coming of humans, and Later Heaven is the world with all the burdens and demands that humans place on the Earth. You may also find that the Former Heaven arrangement is discussed as being appropriate to our ancestors and therefore to grave sites, while the Later Heaven arrangement is appropriate for the living.

Clearly the two arrangements are connected and if you look at them in terms of the directions derived from their association with the seasons, they do not, in fact, contradict one another.

Former Heaven Sequence

This is the arrangement that is seen on the *bagua* or *pa kua* mirrors that are often placed over the front door to ward off negative ch'i. In this arrangement, Heaven, or *chien*, is placed at the top, representing south, and Earth, or *kun*, is placed at the bottom, representing north.

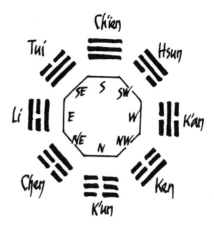

If we begin with Heaven and follow the pattern in a clockwise direction, an interesting pattern emerges, which perfectly imitates the natural order of the seasons.

Heaven is represented as pure yang; this is followed by a yin line appearing at the bottom, followed by two yin lines surrounding the yang line, moving on to the yang line being pushed out at the top, before ending with pure yin. This pattern then repeats itself, beginning with a yang line appearing at the bottom and so on, before ending again with pure yang.

This arrangement depicts the natural flow of ch'i over the course of a year: the summer solstice represents the most yang point of the year, when the days are at their longest and the nights are the shortest. The winter solstice represents the point of the year when the yin energy is at its strongest. This is illustrated by the fact that the Chinese characters that make up the word 'yang' consist of a hill with the sun on it, while a hill with the moon represents the word 'yin'.

East and west are represented as the spring and autumn equinoxes, the points at which day and night, or yin and yang, are equal. The west has a yang line surrounded by two yin lines, depicting the autumn equinox when the yin energy begins to dominate, while in the east we have the reverse, representing the spring equinox.

Later Heaven Sequence

This is the more familiar sequence since this is the arrangement that is most frequently used in the current popular styles of feng shui.

In this arrangement, Fire, or *li*, is placed at the top, representing south, while Water, or *k'an*, is placed at the bottom, representing north. It is interesting to note that these two trigrams were also opposite each other in the previous arrangement, although this parallel does not occur with any other pairs.

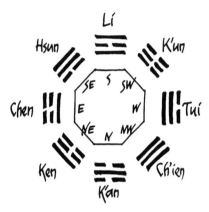

In the Later Heaven arrangement, the elements of the trigrams that represent the four cardinal directions reflect the elements associated with the seasons. Fire, the element of summer is in the South. Metal, the element of autumn, is in the west. Water, the element of winter is in the north. Wood, the element of spring, is in the east.

How the Sequences Relate

From this, we can see that although the two sequences are very different, they also complement one another. Former Heaven expresses the annual cycle in terms of yin and yang, while Later Heaven depicts the same annual cycle but in terms of the elements. In this way, since the elements associated with each of the eight trigrams remain constant in both arrangements, they can be seen as different expressions of the same thing.

It is therefore not surprising that there are styles of feng shui that use calculations which involve both arrangements. This is especially true of the Flying Star schools, in which the styles are differentiated by the combination they use. In Hong Kong, for example, the Sam Hap style of Flying Star feng shui uses the Former Heaven arrangement, while the San Yuan style uses the Later Heaven arrangement and there are others who prefer a combination of the two.

The Eight Houses and the Workplace

For business purposes, the emphasis is placed on the trigrams relating to each area of the office, factory or premises. However, other influences, known as the Eight Houses, which have a secondary importance, are also relevant. These are influences that are associated more closely with the home, so you will find more details of their energies on pages 18–23, but they do also have some relevance to business premises and they are particularly relevant in factories or businesses that may use dangerous machinery or hazardous substances.

Now we are discussing your workplace, this is a reminder of the major features of each aspect of ch'i.

Sheng Ch'i – Source of Ch'i
As the name suggests, this is a very favourable influence, denoting vitality.

Nien Yen – Long Life
Another favourable influence, this relates to long life and lasting relationships.

T'ien I or T'ien Yi – Heavenly Doctor
Another very favourable influence denoting health as well as wealth.

Fu Wei – Bowing to the Throne
Within a building, this area is always situated at the entrance and is also considered to be favourable.

Wu Kuei – Five Ghosts
An unfavourable area, but good for a night watchman because he would be less inclined to sleep.

Liu Sha – Six Curses or Six Imps
Although an unfavourable area, this really implies only minor recurrent annoyances.

Hai Huo – Accidents and Mishaps
Dangerous machinery or hazardous substances should not be placed in this area. If this is unavoidable, extra caution and safety measures should be taken.

Chueh Ming – Broken or Severed Fate
As the name suggests, this is not a favourable area. Try to avoid spending long periods of time here.

The Arrangement of the Eight Houses

The following diagram relates these types of ch'i energy to the Later Heaven arrangement, which is using feng shui in its simplest form. This is an excellent starting-point for understanding the basic principles that are involved and avoiding confusion.

Wu kwei South-east	Lui sha South	Fu wei South-west
Hai huo East		T'ien I West
Sheng ch'i North-east	Chueh ming North	Nien yen North-west

The Elements and Successful Business

風水

In feng shui for business, one of the first things that needs to be determined is the element that is associated with that business. Some companies cover a wide spectrum of activities and if this is the case, each area of the premises can be used most effectively, with distribution, manufacturing, design and leadership all placed in the areas associated with that type of change.

However, in the case of the small business, this is not so. In a local shop, for example, the whole area is related to selling goods, with the possible exception of any storage areas. These businesses need to be treated differently by relating them to an appropriate element.

Many shops or businesses are specialised, dealing in a range of similar items, such as books or food. Others, such as travel agents or banks, sell services rather than goods. It stands to reason, therefore, that activating a restaurant would be very different to activating a car showroom, and in order to differentiate between the two we have to allocate a personal element, just as we do when looking at individuals. Using the principles that govern the five elements, we can look at the business and determine which element is associated with that type of activity. The Chinese classify everything in terms of elements – even nuclear power stations and computer games have been classified as belonging to one element or another.

Some classifications are quite obvious. A swimming pool would belong to the Water element, for example, as would a launderette, which uses water to wash clothes. A bakery, which uses ovens to bake bread and cakes, is obviously a Fire business, since Fire is the heart of the process. Other businesses may not initially be so obvious but elements can be allocated according to recognised principles. In some cases, a business might appear to relate to more than one element, but it is important to isolate the primary function of the business in order to assign an appropriate element.

Wood

Shops that sell wooden objects, like wooden furniture, obviously belong to the Wood element.

Since Wood is associated with spring, which nourishes the new year, Wood is also associated with nourishment and healing, so restaurants, cafés and anything to do with food or catering are all considered to be related to Wood, as are chemists, doctors' surgeries, health centres, health-food shops and hospitals.

Plants also belong to the Wood element, so florists, plant nurseries and also greengrocers are Wood businesses. The growth connection also means that Wood relates to children's nurseries, playgroups and crèches.

Fire

The obvious activities that fit into this category are power stations, foundries, furnaces, bakeries and kitchens, since they all utilise heat and fire. Fire also represents animals, as well as blood, and therefore any establishments connected with livestock, such as abattoirs and butchers' shops, all relate to Fire. It also encompasses businesses manufacturing or selling leather goods, pet shops and blood-donor centres.

Intellect and expression are also associated with Fire; therefore libraries and bookshops belong to this group, along with theatres, colleges, study centres, universities, schools and other places of learning.

Earth

This element is fairly straightforward: it encompasses activities that include building, construction and civil engineering, as well as property development and landscaping. Farming also falls into this category, along with businesses that offer storage of any kind, including safety deposit boxes and vaults.

Metal

Railways, mechanics and breakers' yards would be classified as Metal, along with silversmiths, goldsmiths and jewellers, as the core of their business is involved with Metal.

Metal is the element of money and as a result any business that deals with money is said to belong to this element. Banks, accountants, casinos and betting shops would all fit into this category, along with any businesses providing financial services.

This element is also associated with authority and enforcement, so police stations and courts are also classified as associated with the Metal element.

Water

Swimming pools and spas are the obvious businesses associated with Water but many of the activities that utilise Water or liquids are also associated with this element, so brewing, distilling, glass-making, laundries and oil wells all qualify.

Water is also associated with communication and therefore media, marketing, computers, networking and word-processing all belong to this element. Speech therapy, after-dinner speaking and elocution are also associated with Water.

Music and art also belong to this category, so music shops, art galleries, concert halls and opera houses would also be categorised as related to the Water element.

Using the Workplace Elements

Once you have established the element your business relates to, it is important to try and strengthen this element as much as possible.

If your business is a health-food shop, which relates to the Wood element, the introduction of the Water element will help to strengthen it, since Water is said to generate Wood. Similarly, if your business belongs to the Water element, then you should introduce Metal, since Metal generates Water. Simply use the elemental cycle of generation (see page 10) to guide you in which elements support and strengthen each other.

Elements Relating to the Premises

Once you have determined which element relates to your type of business, you need to calculate the element that relates to the premises, and this is determined by the direction in which they face (see page 12). South-facing premises relate to Fire, while north-facing premises relate to Water. Premises facing east and south-east relate to Wood. Businesses facing south-west and north-east relate to Earth while premises facing north-west and west relate to Metal.

In an ideal world, the element associated with this direction should be in harmony with the element related to your business. Naturally, this will not happen in all cases, so you will need to determine the relationship between the two elements so that you can assess whether the element associated with the premises generates, supports, controls or submits to the element associated with the business.

If the elements are in harmony or mutually supportive, that is a good sign, although it would be far better for the premises to generate the business, rather than the business generating the premises.

However, if things are not in harmony, then you will have to see which element you can introduce to balance the situation, at the same time as trying to generate the element that is associated with the business.

Supporting and Generating the Elements

As an example, let us look again at a health-food shop, which belongs to the Wood element. This would benefit from facing north, since this direction is associated with Water. East or south-east would also be favourable, since these both belong to the Wood element and therefore provide additional support for the Wood business.

If you find that your business is facing one of the least favourable directions – for example where the Wood business is facing west or north-west and is under attack from the Metal element – one way to combat the negative energies would be to introduce a controlling element. If Wood is under threat from Metal, the introduction of Fire would help to control the Metal, and if Water was under threat from Earth, introducing Wood would help to control the Earth.

However, this is not necessarily the best approach as it uses force to combat conflict and therefore the end does not result in harmony and balance. A delightful Chinese proverb illustrates the futility of conflict: 'It is useless to fight evil with evil; after all, although the teeth are stronger, the lips last longer.' With this in mind, it is prudent to look for another approach.

When Wood is under threat from Metal, instead of introducing Fire to control the Metal, introduce Water. This element feeds not only off Metal but it also feeds Wood. Here we have three elements working in harmony: Metal generating Water, which in turn generates Wood. If we had introduced Fire, this would have resulted in Wood generating Fire, which would then destroy the Metal but at the same time the Wood would have been depleted by the Fire so a negative cycle would have been created.

As another example, if Water was under threat from Earth, introducing the Wood element would control the Earth, but since Water feeds Wood, the Water would also be depleted. If we added Metal, then we would have harmony since Earth generates Metal, which in turn generates Water, again creating a generating cycle. Now the Water that was under attack is being regenerated.

Your Pillars of Destiny

風水

ost people know that, in Chinese terms, each individual relates most specifically to one of the elements. Many people who are already familiar with the method of calculating their personal element according to their *kua* number have been confused by finding that they may reach another conclusion if they calculate their element according to nine-star ki. This confusion can be made even worse if you discover other, more complex methods. In a worst-case scenario, you could use five different methods for the same person and get five different answers. Yet the answer to this apparently simple question is crucial because the remedy is based on the answer. It is therefore essential to find a bona fide answer to the question.

All the popularised methods of calculating your personal element are simplified versions based on the same ancient knowledge. They are not 'wrong' but they do provide only part of the picture. There are three areas in which they raise confusion.

Firstly, all methods define a person's element using the time of birth. Most popular methods use the year of birth, but there are also elements relating to the month, day and even the hour of birth, and it is, in fact, the day that is actually the most relevant factor.

Secondly, although all the systems provide a method of calculating which element a person is, none of them provides any indication as to the strength or weakness of that element, which is essential in order to 'treat' it effectively.

Finally, the popular methods assume that everyone is made up of all five elements, a concept that many traditional Chinese feng shui masters would not support. Different people actually have differing balances of the elements within their make-up, sometimes lacking some altogether.

The Importance of the Day Pillars

The Chinese Ten Thousand Year Calendar is the oldest working calendar in use today and it has served the Chinese for nearly 5,000 years. It is unique because it integrates lunar and solar cycles and because, unlike the Western calendar, it expresses time in terms of elements.

According to the Chinese calendar, each unit of time – hour, day, month and year – is associated with an element and with one of 12 animals. Since each of the animals is also associated with a particular element, this results in pairs of elements, or pillars. Each pillar therefore consists of two Chinese characters, one relating to the heavenly stem, or element, and the other to the earthly branch, represented as an animal.

Every hour, day, month and year is expressed as a pillar – an hour pillar, a day pillar, a month pillar and a year pillar – and it is these pillars that traditional Chinese feng shui masters use to determine not only their client's personal element, but also their luck. For example, 6 pm on 14 February 1966 can be expressed as the hour of the Water Rooster, the day of the Wood Dragon, during the month of the Metal Tiger, in the year of the Fire Horse. These are known as the Four Pillars, or the Pillars of Destiny.

The traditional way to determine the most influential personal element is to use the element relating to the heavenly stem from the day pillar. A person born on the day of the Water Rabbit would be a Water person, a person born on the day of the Fire Pig would be a Fire person, someone born on the day of the Earth Monkey, would be an Earth person, and so on.

A final consideration is to remember that although there are only five elements, each element exists as either yin or yang, so a person can either be a yin Wood person or a yang Wood person, irrespective of whether they are male or female.

Having selected the heavenly stem of the day pillar – relating to the hour, month and year – as the person's personal element, there are seven characters remaining, all of which relate to a particular element. From these, the feng shui master can make a full assessment of the strength or weakness of the client's personal element. This information also relates to a person's luck at any given time period, a topic that will be covered later in the book. In addition to this, it provides a greater depth of knowledge on how different people are affected by the energies in a house or workplaces. Finally, it defines your House of Spouse, the method by which the Chinese establish successful relationships.

Calculating Your Day Pillar

風水

Having established the importance of the pillars and, in particular the day pillar, we will now present a method of calculating the day pillar. Most people could not read the Chinese Ten Thousand Year Calendar even if they had access to it, so we need a simple method of determining the stem and branch for any given day, and that is what the three tables on pages 59–60 provide. If you follow the method step by step and look at the examples, you will be surprised how straightforward it is, although it does demand some concentration. The same system applies equally to males and females. While the approach is Westernised, the conclusions are authentic according to the tenets of traditional Chinese feng shui.

Wade first devised a similar system in the nineteenth century and it provides a useful way of determining the day pillar of any given date. Derek Walters simplified the system and, having studied with Derek, I have simplified it even further.

The **Year Table** gives a number for 1 January in any given year, which relates to the combinations for that year; for example, the year 1976 is represented by the number 49. Looking at the Pillar Table on page 60, you will see that 49 is represented as the Yang Water Rat. This means that 1 January 1976 was the Day of the Yang Water Rat.

The **Month Table** provides the monthly variables. January is represented as zero because this is the starting point for which we have already established the combination. For the remaining months, we need to add on from that point, so February is represented as 31 because we have to include the 31 days of January before we consider dates in February.

The **Pillar Table** lists all the 60 combinations, or pillars, in their correct sequence, numbered 1–60 beginning with the Yang Wood Rat and ending with the Yin Water Pig. Once this 60-year sequence has been completed, it begins again with the Yang Wood Rat.

The Pillar Table also shows whether the pillar relates to yin or yang, and an easy way to remember this is that the odd numbers in the table are yang and the even numbers are yin. Another determining factor is that yin stems only combine with yin branches, or animals, and yang stems with yang branches. So if you know the branch, you know the stem must match. Yin branches are: Ox, Rabbit, Snake, Sheep, Rooster and Pig. Yang branches are: Rat, Tiger, Dragon, Horse, Monkey and Dog.

One final important point is to check whether the year is a leap year. If the date falls after 28 February in a leap year, you will have to add one to your calculation. Leap years are divisible by four and are marked with an asterisk in the Year Table, and the step-by-step instructions below explain exactly how to take this into account.

Step 1: Look in the Year Table on page 59 to find the number associated with the year you were born.

Step 2: Look in the Month Table on page 59 to find the number associated with the month you were born.

Step 3: Take the number of the actual day of your birthday and subtract 1.

Step 4: If your birthday is in a leap year and is after 28 February, add 1. If the date is not in a leap year, add nothing.

Step 5: Add all the numbers together. If the number is over 60, subtract 60, and if necessary another 60, in order to arrive at a figure of 60 or less.

Step 6: Look up that number in the Pillar Table on page 60 to find your personal day pillar.

Example A: Finding the day pillar for 27 October 1963

Step 1: Look up 1963 in the Year Table.	41
Step 2: Look up October in the Month Table.	33
Step 3: Take the date and subtract 1.	27 – 1 = 26
Step 4: 1963 was not a leap year, so add zero.	0
Step 5: Add these numbers together.	100
Step 6: Subtract 60 to reduce to a number of 60 or less.	40
Step 7: Look up 40 in the Pillar Table.	Yin Water Rabbit

A person born on 27 October 1963 is a yin Water person.

Example B: Finding the day pillar for 14 March 1952

Step 1: Look up 1952 in the Year Table.	43
Step 2: Look up March in the Month Table.	59
Step 3: Take the date and subtract 1.	14 – 1 = 13
Step 4: 1952 was a leap year and 14 March was after 28 February, so add 1.	1
Step 5: Add these numbers together.	116
Step 6: Subtract 60 to reduce to a number of 60 or less.	56
Step 7: Look up 56 in table 3.	Yin Earth Sheep

A person born on 14 March 1952 is a yin Earth person.

Example C: Finding the day pillar for 18 January 1988
Step 1: Look up 1988 in the Year Table.   52
Step 2: Look up January in the Month Table.   0
Step 3: Take the date and subtract 1.   18 – 1 = 17
Step 4: 1988 was a leap year but 18 January was
    before 28 February, so add zero.   0
Step 5: Add these numbers together.   69
Step 6: Subtract 60 to reduce to a number 60 or less.   9
Step 7: Look up 9 in the Pillar Table.   Yang Water Monkey
A person born on 18 January 1988 is a yang Water person.

YEAR TABLE: The Yearly Variables

1900*	10	1921	1	1942	51	1963	41	1984*	31
1901	16	1922	6	1943	56	1964*	46	1985	37
1902	21	1923	11	1944*	1	1965	52	1986	42
1903	26	1924*	16	1945	7	1966	57	1987	47
1904*	31	1925	22	1946	12	1967	2	1988*	52
1905	37	1926	27	1947	17	1968*	7	1989	58
1906	42	1927	32	1948*	22	1969	13	1990	3
1907	47	1928*	37	1949	28	1970	18	1991	8
1908*	52	1929	43	1950	33	1971	23	1992*	13
1909	58	1930	48	1951	38	1972*	28	1993	19
1910	3	1931	53	1952*	43	1973	34	1994	24
1911	8	1932*	58	1953	49	1974	39	1995	29
1912*	13	1933	4	1954	54	1975	44	1996*	34
1913	19	1934	9	1955	59	1976*	49	1997	40
1914	24	1935	14	1956*	4	1977	55	1998	45
1915	29	1936*	19	1957	10	1978	60	1999	50
1916*	34	1937	25	1958	15	1979	5	2000*	55
1917	40	1938	30	1959	20	1980*	10	2001	1
1918	45	1939	35	1960*	25	1981	16	2002	6
1919	50	1940*	40	1961	31	1982	21	2003	11
1920*	55	1941	46	1962	36	1983	26	2004*	16

MONTH TABLE: The Monthly Variables

January	0	May	0	September	3
February	31	June	31	October	33
March	59	July	1	November	4
April	30	August	32	December	34

PILLAR TABLE: The Combinations of Stems and Branches

1	Yang Wood Rat	21	Yang Wood Monkey	41	Yang Wood Dragon
2	Yin Wood Ox	22	Yin Wood Rooster	42	Yin Wood Snake
3	Yang Fire Tiger	23	Yang Fire Dog	43	Yang Fire Horse
4	Yin Fire Rabbit	24	Yin Fire Pig	44	Yin Fire Sheep
5	Yang Earth Dragon	25	Yang Earth Rat	45	Yang Earth Monkey
6	Yin Earth Snake	26	Yin Earth Ox	46	Yin Earth Rooster
7	Yang Metal Horse	27	Yang Metal Tiger	47	Yang Metal Dog
8	Yin Metal Sheep	28	Yin Metal Rabbit	48	Yin Metal Pig
9	Yang Water Monkey	29	Yang Water Dragon	49	Yang Water Rat
10	Yin Water Rooster	30	Yin Water Snake	50	Yin Water Ox
11	Yang Wood Dog	31	Yang Wood Horse	51	Yang Wood Tiger
12	Yin Wood Pig	32	Yin Wood Sheep	52	Yin Wood Rabbit
13	Yang Fire Rat	33	Yang Fire Monkey	53	Yang Fire Dragon
14	Yin Fire Ox	34	Yin Fire Rooster	54	Yin Fire Snake
15	Yang Earth Tiger	35	Yang Earth Dog	55	Yang Earth Horse
16	Yin Earth Rabbit	36	Yin Earth Pig	56	Yin Earth Sheep
17	Yang Metal Dragon	37	Yang Metal Rat	57	Yang Metal Monkey
18	Yin Metal Snake	38	Yin Metal Ox	58	Yin Metal Rooster
19	Yang Water Horse	39	Yang Water Tiger	59	Yang Water Dog
20	Yin Water Sheep	40	Yin Water Rabbit	60	Yin Water Pig

You have now calculated your day pillar, which is arguably the most important as the stem represents your personal element, or Day Master, while the branch represents your Marriage Palace, or House of Spouse. You now know that you were born on the day of the Yang Water Horse, for example, in which case you are a yang Water person, and this will open your eyes to a whole new area of understanding. You will find out exactly how to use this knowledge to improve your life and relationships in the following chapters.

Calculating Your Year Pillar

風水

The day pillar is the most crucial for many Chinese calculations, but it is also useful to know your year, month and hour pillars so that you can be more accurate in your assessments of the energies relating to your life. The next few sections show you how to calculate your pillars and construct a table of all your pillars.

Calculating the Year Pillars

The Chinese New Year does not begin at the same time as the Western year, and there are three possible methods of calculating when it falls. Some say the new year begins on the second new moon after the winter solstice, which falls at the end of January or the beginning of February. Some use the winter solstice itself, a solar calculation that represents the point at which the yin energy has reached its peak – with the day at its shortest point and the night at its longest – and the seed of yang begins to grow. Most, however, use the *Li Chun* spring festival as the beginning of the year, another solar calculation since it relates to one of the 24 solar ch'i (see pages 69–70). This takes place on either 4 or 5 February.

The table on page 62 shows the stem and branch pillars for 1900–2004. Those years when the Li Chun festival falls on 4 February are marked with an asterisk; those years when the festival falls on 5 February are not marked. The pillars are represented in numerical terms, so once you have looked up the number for the year in question, refer to the Pillar Table on page 60 to see which pillar that number relates to. If you are calculating a date in January, or one that falls before the Li Chun festival, you will need to use the stem and branch of the previous year.

YEAR TABLE: The Stem and Branch for 1 January									
1900*	37	1921*	58	1942*	19	1963*	40	1984*	01
1901*	38	1922*	59	1943	20	1964	41	1985*	02
1902	39	1923	60	1944	21	1965*	42	1986*	03
1903	40	1924	01	1945*	22	1966*	43	1987*	04
1904	41	1925*	02	1946*	23	1967*	44	1988*	05
1905*	42	1926*	03	1947*	24	1968	45	1989*	06
1906	43	1927	04	1948	25	1969*	46	1990*	07
1907	44	1928	05	1949*	26	1970*	47	1991*	08
1908	45	1929*	06	1950*	27	1971*	48	1992*	09
1909*	46	1930*	07	1951*	28	1972	49	1993*	10
1910	47	1931	08	1952	29	1973*	50	1994*	11
1911	48	1932	09	1953*	30	1974*	51	1995*	12
1912	49	1933*	10	1954*	31	1975*	52	1996*	13
1913*	50	1934*	11	1955*	32	1976	53	1997*	14
1914*	51	1935	12	1956	33	1977*	54	1998*	15
1915	52	1936	13	1957*	34	1978*	55	1999*	16
1916	53	1937*	14	1958*	35	1979*	56	2000*	17
1917*	54	1938*	15	1959*	36	1980	57	2001*	18
1918*	55	1939	16	1960	37	1981*	58	2002*	19
1919	56	1940	17	1961*	38	1982*	59	2003*	20
1920	57	1941*	18	1962*	39	1983*	60	2004*	21

Example A: Finding the year pillar for 7 October 1972

Step 1: The date falls after the Li Chun festival, so look for 1972 on the table above: 49.

Step 2: Refer to the Pillar Table on page 60 to find that 49 represents the Yang Water Rat.

Example B: Finding the year pillar for January 28 1935

Step 1: The date falls before the Li Chun festival, so look for 1934 on the table above: 11.

Step 2: Refer to the Pillar Table on page 60 to find that 11 represents the Yang Wood Dog.

Calculating Your Month Pillar

風水

To calculate the branch of the month pillar, refer to the table below. Note that the Chinese months do not begin on the same day as Western months.

WESTERN MONTH	EARTHLY BRANCH	WESTERN MONTH	EARTHLY BRANCH
5/6 January	Ox	7/8 July	Sheep
4/5 February	Tiger	7/8 August	Monkey
5/6 March	Rabbit	7/8 September	Rooster
4/5 April	Dragon	8/9 October	Dog
5/6 May	Snake	7/8 November	Pig
5/6 June	Horse	7/8 December	Rat

For example, if you are looking for the branch pillar for 18 October, since this is after 8/9 October, it would be the Dog. The branch pillar for 2 February, since it is before 4/5 February, would be the Ox.

Having determined the branch, you then need to calculate the stem from the table on page 64, which is commonly referred to as 'five tigers chasing the month' because it does not use the traditional sequence, beginning with the Rat, but uses the Tiger, emphasising the beginning of the year. The Tiger month begins on the day of the Li Chun spring festival. There is a special relationship between the year and the month.

Step 1: Take the branch of the month that you have just calculated.

Step 2: Take the number of the stem of the year pillar from the Year Table above, then relate that number to the Pillar Table on page 60.

Step 3: Find the branch in the left-hand column of the table on page 64, then find the stem of the year pillar in the first horizontal row. Where the column and row intersect gives you the month pillar.

An associated element is given in brackets beneath the pairs of year stems. Yang Wood and Yin Earth are said to combine and this combination produces Earth. Yin Wood and Yang Metal combine to produce Metal, and so on. If you can remember the pairs and their associated element and you can also remember that the stem of the month of the Tiger is the element that generates this element, you won't need to use this table, since everything else follows in sequence. For example, in a year with a stem of yang Metal, yang Metal combines with yin Wood to produce Metal. Since Earth generates Metal, the stem of the month of the Tiger in that year must be Earth. The Tiger is considered to be yang; therefore the stem must be yang Earth.

Five Tigers Chasing the Month

MONTH BRANCH	YEAR STEMS: Yang Wood and Yin Earth (Earth)	YEAR STEMS: Yin Wood and Yang Metal (Metal)	YEAR STEMS: Yang Fire and Yin Metal (Water)	YEAR STEMS: Yin Fire and Yang Wood (Wood)	YEAR STEMS: Yang Earth and Yin Water (Fire)
Tiger	Yang Fire	Yang Earth	Yang Metal	Yang Water	Yang Wood
Rabbit	Yin Fire	Yin Earth	Yin Metal	Yin Water	Yin Wood
Dragon	Yang Earth	Yang Metal	Yang Water	Yang Wood	Yang Fire
Snake	Yin Earth	Yin Metal	Yin Water	Yin Wood	Yin Fire
Horse	Yang Metal	Yang Water	Yang Wood	Yang Fire	Yang Earth
Sheep	Yin Metal	Yin Water	Yin Wood	Yin Fire	Yin Earth
Monkey	Yang Water	Yang Wood	Yang Fire	Yang Earth	Yang Metal
Rooster	Yin Water	Yin Wood	Yin Fire	Yin Earth	Yin Metal
Dog	Yang Wood	Yang Fire	Yang Earth	Yang Metal	Yang Water
Pig	Yin Wood	Yin Fire	Yin Earth	Yin Metal	Yin Water
Rat	Yang Fire	Yang Earth	Yang Metal	Yang Water	Yang Wood
Ox	Yin Fire	Yin Earth	Yin Metal	Yin Water	Yin Wood

Example A: Finding the stem of the month of the Rat in 1965

Step 1: The branch is the Rat.

Step 2: The stem of the year pillar for 1965 in the table above is 42. Look this up in the Pillar Table on page 60 to find that it relates to Yin Wood Snake.

Step 3: Find the Rat in the left-hand column. Find Yin Wood year stems in the first row. Where the row and column intersect gives the month stem: Yang Earth. The month pillar for the Rat in 1965 is therefore Yang Earth Rat.

Calculating Your Hour Pillar

風水

To calculate the hour pillar, we use a similar approach, as when we calculated the other pillars. First work out the hour branch, then use the day stem, rather than the year stem, to work out the hour stem.

WESTERN HOURS	EARTHLY BRANCH	WESTERN HOURS	EARTHLY BRANCH
11 pm–1 am	Rat	11 am–1 pm	Horse
1 am–3 am	Ox	1 pm–3 pm	Sheep
3 am–5 am	Tiger	3 pm–5 pm	Monkey
5 am–7 am	Rabbit	5 pm–7 pm	Rooster
7 am–9 am	Dragon	7 pm–9 pm	Dog
9 am–11 am	Snake	9 pm–11 pm	Pig

Step 1: Work out the hour branch by referring to the table above. For example, 6.30 pm falls between 6 and 7 pm, so the hour branch is the Rooster.

Step 2: Look up this branch in the left-hand column of the table overleaf. Look up the day stem in the first horizontal row. Where the column and row intersect, you will find the hour stem.

Five Rats Chasing the Clock

HOUR BRANCH	DAY STEMS: Yang Wood and Yin Earth (Earth)	DAY STEMS: Yin Wood and Yang Metal (Metal)	DAY STEMS: Yang Fire and Yin Metal (Water)	DAY STEMS: Yin Fire and Yang Wood (Wood)	DAY STEMS: Yang Earth and Yin Water (Fire)
Rat	Yang Wood	Yang Fire	Yang Earth	Yang Metal	Yang Water
Ox	Yin Wood	Yin Fire	Yin Earth	Yin Metal	Yin Water
Tiger	Yang Fire	Yang Earth	Yang Metal	Yang Water	Yang Wood
Rabbit	Yin Fire	Yin Earth	Yin Metal	Yin Water	Yin Wood
Dragon	Yang Earth	Yang Metal	Yang Water	Yang Wood	Yang Fire
Snake	Yin Earth	Yin Metal	Yin Water	Yin Wood	Yin Fire
Horse	Yang Metal	Yang Water	Yang Wood	Yang Fire	Yang Earth
Sheep	Yin Metal	Yin Water	Yin Wood	Yin Fire	Yin Earth
Monkey	Yang Water	Yang Wood	Yang Fire	Yang Earth	Yang Metal
Rooster	Yin Water	Yin Wood	Yin Fire	Yin Earth	Yin Metal
Dog	Yang Wood	Yang Fire	Yang Earth	Yang Metal	Yang Water
Pig	Yin Wood	Yin Fire	Yin Earth	Yin Metal	Yin Water

For example, for the Ox hour on a day with a yin Fire stem, the row and column intersect at yin Metal.

Again, if you can remember the combinations of stems and their associated element, and you can remember that the hour of the Rat is associated with the element that controls that element, you will soon not need to refer to the chart. For example, on a day with the stem of yang Wood, which is paired with yin Earth and produces Earth, the Rat has the stem of Wood, since Wood is said to control Earth.

Constructing a Chart for Your Pillars

風水

You will need to adopt a methodical approach when working out a set of pillars, and use the format below to record the information. First find the day pillar, then the year, then the month and finally the hour. The following examples recap all the calculations you have been making over the previous chapters so that you can practise the system.

	HOUR PILLAR	DAY PILLAR	MONTH PILLAR	YEAR PILLAR
Heavenly Stem				
Earthly Branch				

Finding the pillars for a female born on 18 July 1966 at 3.45 pm

Day pillar
Step 1: Look in the Year Table on page 59 to find the number associated with the year: 57.

Step 2: Look in the Month Table on page 59 to find the number associated with the month: 1.

Step 3: Take the number of the actual date and subtract 1: 18 − 1 = 17.

Step 4: Since it is not a leap year, add 0.

Step 5: Add all the numbers together = 75. Subtract 60 = 15.

Step 6: Look up 15 in the Pillar Table on page 60 to find the day pillar: Yang Earth Tiger. Write this in the table.

	HOUR PILLAR	DAY PILLAR	MONTH PILLAR	YEAR PILLAR
Heavenly Stem		Yang Earth		
Earthly Branch		Tiger		

Year pillar
Step 1: The date falls after the Li Chun festival, so look for 1966 on the table on page 62: 43.

Step 2: Refer to the Pillar Table on page 60 to find that 43 represents the Yang Fire Horse. Write this into the chart.

	HOUR PILLAR	DAY PILLAR	MONTH PILLAR	YEAR PILLAR
Heavenly Stem		Yang Earth		Yang Fire
Earthly Branch		Tiger		Horse

Month pillar

Step 1: Take the branch for a date in July after 7/8: Sheep.

Step 2: The year pillar has already been defined as yang Fire.

Step 3: Find the branch in the left-hand column of the table on page 64, then find the stem of the year pillar in the first horizontal row. Where the column and row intersect gives you the month pillar: yin Wood. Write this in the table.

	HOUR PILLAR	DAY PILLAR	MONTH PILLAR	YEAR PILLAR
Heavenly Stem		Yang Earth	Yin Wood	Yang Fire
Earthly Branch		Tiger	Sheep	Horse

Hour pillar

Step 1: Refer to the table on page 65 to find that the hour branch is Monkey.

Step 2: Look up Monkey in the left-hand column of the table on page 66. The day stem has already been defined as yang Earth. Look this up in the first horizontal row. Where the column and row intersect, you will find the hour stem: Yang Metal. Write this in to complete the chart.

	HOUR PILLAR	DAY PILLAR	MONTH PILLAR	YEAR PILLAR
Heavenly Stem	Yang Metal	Yang Earth	Yin Wood	Yang Fire
Earthly Branch	Monkey	Tiger	Sheep	Horse

Evaluating the Strength of Your Personal Element

風水

The seasons are important for many reasons, but for our purposes they provide a valuable insight into the strength or weakness of our personal element. This table relates to the personal element in your day pillar. Each season is associated with an element. Someone whose seasonal element and personal element are the same will be most strongly influenced by that element. For example, a Wood person born during spring, the season of Wood, is influenced more strongly by this element than a Wood person born in autumn, the season of Metal. This is because the five elements flow over the course of the year in harmony with the generating and controlling cycles. Through the seasons, each element is said to be born, flourish, rest, weaken and die in an ever-changing cycle. When one element is flourishing, the element it controls is said to be dying. For example, a Fire person is said to be flourishing in the summer, while a Metal person would be said to be dying.

ELEMENT	BORN	FLOURISHES	RESTS	WEAKENS	DIES
Relative Strength	√√√	√√√√	√√√	√√	√
Wood	Winter	Spring	Summer	Earth season	Autumn
Fire	Spring	Summer	Earth season	Autumn	Winter
Earth	Summer	Earth season	Autumn	Winter	Spring
Metal	Earth season	Autumn	Winter	Spring	Summer
Water	Autumn	Winter	Spring	Summer	Earth season

The Chinese Seasons

Although the Chinese calendar is now primarily based on lunar cycles, it still incorporates the ancient calendar, which measures the seasons by solar cycles. These are known as the 24 solar ch'i and they are used to calculate the months, the winter and summer solstices and the spring and summer equinoxes. Some people calculate the month using lunar cycles, and this causes confusion because in the Chinese lunar calendar some years have 13 months. Using the solar ch'i to determine the month is not only more authentic, it is also more logical because although the moon controls the tides, the sun controls the seasons.

As we have seen in the Chinese calendar, there are four main seasons plus four Earth seasons, each of which consists of the last 18 days of the main seasons: the last 18 days of spring, the last 18 days of summer, and so on. The Earth season is often called 'the four season' in China because it arrives four times a year, so there is a spring Earth season, a summer Earth season, an autumn Earth season and a winter Earth season. The four Earth seasons are balancing periods, during which we can prepare ourselves for each coming season. In this way, each of the five elements is said to influence roughly 73 days.

Using the table below, you will be able to determine the season in which you were born. You can then consider how this affects your personal element and whether you want to take any measures to strengthen or control any of the elements involved. For example, if you are a yang Wood person born during the spring, you can generally say that you are 'strong Wood'. If you are an Earth person born in the spring, your personal element is said to be dying, in which case it may need to be strengthened. You will also see from the charts that each month is represented by an animal – February by the Tiger, March by the Rabbit and so on – and that each animal is also associated with one of the five elements.

SEASON	DATES	ANIMAL	YIN/YANG ELEMENT
Spring	4–5 February to 4–5 March	Tiger	Yang Wood
	5–6 March to 4–5 April	Rabbit	Yin Wood
	5–6 April to 4–5 May	Dragon	Yang Earth
Spring Earth	18–19 April to 4–5 May		
Summer	5–6 May to 4–5 June	Snake	Yin Fire
	5–6 June to 6–7 July	Horse	Yang Fire
	7–8 July to 6–7 August	Sheep	Yin Earth
Summer Earth	20–21 July to 6–7 August		
Autumn	7–8 August to 6–7 September	Monkey	Yang Metal
	7–8 September to 7–8 October	Rooster	Yin Metal
	8–9 October to 6–7 November	Dog	Yang Earth
Autumn Earth	21–22 October to 6–7 November		
Winter	7–8 November to 6–7 December	Pig	Yin Water
	7–8 December to 4–5 January	Rat	Yang Water
	5–6 January to 3–4 February	Ox	Yin Earth
Winter Earth	17–18 January to 3–4 February		

The Hidden Stems

You can delve even deeper by revealing the hidden stems that relate to your four pillars.

The elements associated with the heavenly stems are obvious, but the earthly branches may contain more than one element. These are called the hidden stems, and identifying these enables us to make an evaluation of all the elements that the pillars contain.

The table of hidden stems

EARTHLY BRANCHES	HIDDEN STEMS
Rat	Yin Water
Ox	Yin Earth (major) Yin Water (minor) Yin Metal (tomb)
Tiger	Yang Wood (major) Yang Fire (minor) Yang Earth (minor)
Rabbit	Yin Wood
Dragon	Yang Earth (major) Yin Wood (minor) Yin Water (tomb)
Snake	Yang Fire (major) Yang Metal (minor) Yang Earth (minor)
Horse	Yin Fire (major) Yin Earth (minor)
Sheep	Yin Earth (major) Yin Fire (minor) Yin Wood (tomb)
Monkey	Yang Metal (major) Yang Water (minor) Yang Earth (minor)
Rooster	Yin Metal
Dog	Yang Earth (major) Yin Metal (minor) Yin Fire (tomb)
Pig	Yang Water (major) Yang Wood (minor)

In order to see how these work, let us look at an example by using a male who was born on 20 February 1959 at 4.25 pm. These would be his four pillars, with the hidden stems in place.

HOUR PILLAR	DAY PILLAR	YANG FIRE	YIN EARTH
Yang Metal	Yin Water	Yang Fire	Yin Earth
Monkey	Rooster	Tiger	Pig
HIDDEN STEMS	HIDDEN STEMS	HIDDEN STEMS	HIDDEN STEMS
Yang Metal (major)	Yin Metal (major)	Yang Wood (major)	Yang Water (major)
Yang Water (minor)		Yang Fire (minor)	Yang Wood (minor)
Yang Earth (minor)		Yang Earth (minor)	

The chart shows 12 stems plus the day stem. Three stems are Metal (all major), two stems are Water (one major, one minor), two stems are Wood (one major, one minor), two stems are Fire (one major, one minor) and three stems are Earth (one major, two minor). There are therefore seven major stems and five minor stems, giving a fairly balanced chart. Since we evaluate the elements from a seasonal point of view, the three Metal stems are stronger than the three Earth stems, as Metal is stronger than Earth in spring.

Using the basic principles of the five elements, we know that Metal is said to generate Water, while Earth is said to control Water. As this man is a Water person, it is obviously good that his Metal is stronger than his Earth. In the spring, Wood is at its strongest, and since Wood is said to deplete Water, it is good that he only has two Wood stems, of which only one is a major stem. The Wood is stronger than his Water, but this is balanced out by the fact that Metal generates Water and helps to control Wood.

For this man, Water and Metal would be favourable elements. As his personal element Water is not particularly strong, the Earth element would weaken him so this would be unfavourable. In the controlling cycle, Fire attacks Metal, his favourable element, and it also generates Earth, an unfavourable element, so this would not be particularly good. Wood is a double-edged sword, because although it drains Water, it also helps to control Earth so when the man is in a favourable cycle, Wood could be favourable because it provides a positive outlet for his Water.

Balance is the key and in an ideal world all five elements would flow in harmony. It is no good having a very strong personal element if it cannot flow, much in the same way that we use the expression, 'all dressed up and nowhere to go'. The personal element needs to find a positive outlet, as well as receiving support and encouragement.

Now you have a good assessment of both your own personal element and of the season in which you were born. In the following chapters we will use the information obtained from the tables to examine the effects that the elements have upon each of us at home, at work and in our relationships.

Personal Feng Shui in the Home

風水

In the earlier chapters you established both the portents and the elemental influences in the varous areas of your home. Now you know your personal element and your seasonal element, you have all the information you need to consider your unique, personal feng shui. The most important thing to remember is that you are trying to assess the areas of the home that are most favourable to you, and to use them as much as possible. So, if you are a Wood person and the *sheng ch'i* area of your home is in the east or south-east, associated with Wood, this is very favourable and you should use those sections of the house as main rooms. On the other hand, if you are a Metal person and you live in a house where *sheng ch'i* is located in the south, a Fire area, this is not beneficial. In this case, you need personal feng shui in order to learn how to tap into the source of ch'i without getting burnt.

Controlling Elements

One of the most common remedies is to introduce a controlling element. This is not an element that 'controls' in the usual sense – as when Fire controls Metal – but one that has the ability to balance the situation. In the example I gave above of a Metal person living in a house where *sheng ch'i* is in a Fire area, the resulting conflict has to be replaced with harmony. To achieve this harmony, you introduce Earth to resolve the conflict between Fire and Metal. The Fire can then generate the Earth instead of attacking the Metal, and the Earth can generate the Metal, which was previously under attack from Fire.

In the same way, a Wood person may wish to use the *chueh ming*, or broken fate, area of their home, which is situated in a Metal area. In this case the influence of both the portent and the element are negative. However, introducing Water as the 'controlling' element helps to resolve the situation. Metal attacks Wood but generates Water, which in turn generates Wood. Not only will Water support the Wood person and prevent the Metal from attacking them, it will also help to deplete the negative aspects of the portent, since Water drains Metal.

Elements can be introduced in the form of colours, shapes, designs and images as well as materials. Introducing Earth can be as simple as painting the room yellow and any area can be made Metal by simply painting it white. Look back at the chart on page 12 for ideas.

If you are a Fire person sleeping in an area associated with Water and *sheng ch'i*, the source of ch'i, you are making use of the favourable heavenly influence in the form of the portent, but you are in conflict with the earthly influence, represented by the Water element. By simply painting the room green, to represent Wood, you are now in harmony with both. Instead of the Water attacking your Fire, it will generate the Wood, represented by the new green paint, which in turn will generate you and, as a result, your *sheng ch'i* is improved.

This is the essence of feng shui, the art of balancing the elements to enable us to live in harmony with our environment. The information you have gained so far will help you start to put that balance into effect. The personal guide over the next few pages looks at the various areas in each of the eight houses and shows how they affect you as an individual. Although it is simple and accessible, I have tried to make it as comprehensive as possible.

Water People at Home

風水

This chapter will show Water people how to make the best use of the energies in the home.

Water male

WATER	SELF	FRIENDS	COMPETITORS
Wood	Expression	Career	Positive outlets
Fire	Wealth	Conquests	Spouse
Earth	Pressure	Status	Children and father
Metal	Resources	Support	Mother

Water female

WATER	SELF	FRIENDS	COMPETITORS
Wood	Children	Career	Positive outlets
Fire	Wealth	Conquests	Father
Earth	Pressure	Status	Spouse
Metal	Resources	Support	Mother

The charts above reflect the way the five elements work. As a Water person, Fire represents your wealth, since Water is said to control Fire. Your resources and support are associated with Metal, since Metal is said to generate Water. Wood represents your career and the way you express yourself, since Water creates Wood, and Earth represents pressure, since Earth is said to control Water. When our personal element is strong and we are under the influence of favourable elements, we can overcome obstacles more easily. By coping well with adversity, we not only become stronger but also acquire credibility, acknowledgement and respect that bring greater status. As the Chinese proverb says, 'The measure of success is how well you fare during bad times.'

HOUSE FACING SOUTH		
Chueh ming Broken fate	Nien yen Long life	Hai huo Accidents
Wu kuei Five ghosts		Sheng ch'i Source of ch'i
Liu sha Six curses	Fu wei Bowing to the throne ↓ South	T'ien I Heavenly doctor

Long Life is well placed but could be supported further with Water. Source of Ch'i and Heavenly Doctor are not ideal and would also benefit from the support of Water. The influence of Accidents and Six Curses can be diminished by the introduction of Metal. Broken Fate and Five Ghosts are located in favourable areas but can be improved further with Water.

HOUSE FACING SOUTH-WEST		
Chueh ming Broken fate	Sheng ch'i Source of ch'i	Hai huo Accidents
Nien yen Long life		Wu kuei Five ghosts
T'ien I Heavenly doctor	Fu wei Bowing to the throne ↓ South-west	Liu sha Six curses

Long Life and Heavenly Doctor are both well placed; harness these further with Water. Metal should be introduced to utilise Source of Ch'i. The influence of Five Ghosts and Accidents can both be diminished with the introduction of Fire. Broken Fate and Six Curses are both in favourable areas and it is difficult to advise further improvements.

HOUSE FACING WEST		
Nien yen Long life	*Chueh ming* Broken fate	*Liu sha* Six curses
Hai huo Accidents		*Wu kuei* Five ghosts
Sheng ch'i Source of ch'i	*Fu wei* Bowing to the throne ↓ West	*T'ien I* Heavenly doctor

Source of Ch'i is very well placed but could be harnessed further with Water. Metal is required to utilise Long Life and Heavenly Doctor. To reduce the effects of Broken Fate and Six Curses, introduce Fire. Since Five Ghosts and Accidents both appear in favourable areas, it is difficult to offer general advice to make further improvements.

HOUSE FACING NORTH-WEST		
Wu kuei Five ghosts	*Hai huo* Accidents	*Chueh ming* Broken fate
T'ien I Heavenly doctor		*Nien yen* Long life
Liu sha Six curses	*Fu wei* Bowing to the throne ↓ North-west	*Sheng ch'i* Source of ch'i

Source of Ch'i is ideally placed but you could use Water to harness the energies further. Long Life and Heavenly Doctor will need the introduction of Metal to make them accessible. To diminish the negative influence of Five Ghosts and Accidents, introduce the Fire element. Broken Fate and Six Curses are both located in favourable areas and it is difficult to offer advice that would improve this.

HOUSE FACING NORTH		
Sheng ch'i Source of ch'i	*Nien yen* Long life	*Chueh ming* Broken fate
T'ien I Heavenly doctor		*Hai huo* Accidents
Wu kuei Five ghosts	*Fu wei* Bowing to the throne ↓ North	*Liu sha* Six curses

Source of Ch'i and Heavenly Doctor are not in ideal positions and the
support of Water is needed. Long Life is fairly favourable and difficult to
improve. The influence of Broken Fate and Five Ghosts can be neutralised by
the addition of the Metal element. Accidents and Six Curses appear in
favourable areas but negative energies can be reduced further with the
introduction of Water.

HOUSE FACING NORTH-EAST		
Hai huo Accidents	*Sheng ch'i* Source of ch'i	*Nien yen* Long life
Chueh ming Broken fate		*T'ien I* Heavenly doctor
Liu sha Six curses	*Fu wei* Bowing to the throne ↓ North-east	*Wu kuei* Five ghosts

Source of Ch'i will require Metal to make it accessible. Heavenly Doctor and
Long Life are ideally placed, although they can be harnessed even more with
Water. Introduce Fire to dilute the influence of Broken Fate and Six Curses.
Accidents and Five Ghosts are both located in favourable areas and as a
result it is difficult to advise any further improvements.

HOUSE FACING EAST		
Hai huo Accidents	Chueh ming Broken fate	Wu kuei Five ghosts
Sheng ch'i Source of ch'i		T'ien I Heavenly doctor
Nien yen Long life	Fu wei Bowing to the throne ↓ East	Liu sha Six curses

Heavenly Doctor is well placed but would benefit further with additional Water. Source of Ch'i is reasonably favourable and difficult to improve. Long Life is not ideal and would benefit from the support of Fire. Accidents and Six Curses can be neutralised with Metal. Broken Fate and Five Ghosts are in favourable areas and difficult to improve. However, the addition of the Water element will help to balance the negative aspects.

HOUSE FACING SOUTH-EAST		
Liu sha Six curses	Hai huo Accidents	Sheng ch'i Source of ch'i
Wu kuei Five ghosts		Chueh ming Broken fate
T'ien I Heavenly doctor	Fu wei Bowing to the throne ↓ South-east	Nien yen Long life

Source of Ch'i is well placed but can be enhanced further with Water. Heavenly Doctor is reasonably placed and is difficult to improve. Long Life is not ideal but the introduction of Fire will help. Broken Fate and Five Ghosts can be diminished by the introduction of Metal. Accidents and Six Curses are both in favourable areas but their influence can be diminished even further with Water.

Wood People at Home

風水

This chapter will show Wood people how to make the best use of the energies in the home.

Wood male

WOOD	SELF	FRIENDS	COMPETITORS
Fire	Expression	Career	Positive outlets
Earth	Wealth	Conquests	Spouse
Metal	Pressure	Status	Children and father
Water	Resources	Support	Mother

Wood female

WOOD	SELF	FRIENDS	COMPETITORS
Fire	Children	Career	Positive outlets
Earth	Wealth	Conquests	Father
Metal	Pressure	Status	Spouse
Water	Resources	Support	Mother

The charts above imitate the way the five elements work. As a Wood person, your wealth is represented by Earth, since Wood is said to control Earth. Your resources and support are associated with Water, since Water is said to generate Wood. Fire represents your career and the way you express yourself, since Wood creates Fire. Metal is associated with pressure, since Metal is said to control Wood. When we are strong, we can handle pressure; in this way we acquire status (see page 75).

HOUSE FACING SOUTH		
Chueh ming Broken fate	Nien yen Long life	Hai huo Accidents
Wu kuei Five ghosts		Sheng ch'i Source of ch'i
Liu sha Six curses	Fu wei Bowing to the throne ↓ South	T'ien I Heavenly doctor

Long Life is ideally placed, but you can harness it further by introducing Wood. Heavenly Doctor and Source of Ch'i are both in your element but would benefit from additional Water. The influence of Broken Fate and Five Ghosts can be diminished by the introduction of Water. Accidents and Six Curses are both in favourable areas and are difficult to improve.

HOUSE FACING SOUTH-WEST		
Chueh ming Broken fate	Sheng ch'i Source of ch'i	Hai huo Accidents
Nien yen Long life		Wu kuei Five ghosts
T'ien I Heavenly doctor	Fu wei Bowing to the throne ↓ South-west	Liu sha Six curses

Long Life and Heavenly Doctor are not ideal but can both be made more accessible by the introduction of Water. Source of Ch'i is fairly well placed and difficult to improve. To dilute the effects of Broken Fate, introduce Wood. To reduce the effects of Six Curses, introduce Earth. Accidents and Five Ghosts are both in your element, which reduces their negativity.

HOUSE FACING WEST		
Nien yen Long life	*Chueh ming* Broken fate	*Liu sha* Six curses
Hai huo Accidents		*Wu kuei* Five ghosts
Sheng ch'i Source of ch'i	*Fu wei* Bowing to the throne ↓ West	*T'ien I* Heavenly doctor

Source of Ch'i is not ideal but the introduction of Water will act as peacemaker. Long Life and Heavenly Doctor are fairly auspicious and difficult to improve. The influence of Accidents can be neutralised by Wood and Five Ghosts modfied with Earth. Broken Fate and Six Curses are in your element, which reduces their negativity, and it is difficult to make further improvements.

HOUSE FACING NORTH-WEST		
Wu kuei Five ghosts	*Hai huo* Accidents	*Chueh ming* Broken fate
T'ien I Heavenly doctor		*Nien yen* Long life
Liu sha Six curses	*Fu wei* Bowing to the throne ↓ North-west	*Sheng ch'i* Source of ch'i

Long Life and Heavenly Doctor are reasonably placed and difficult to improve. Source of Ch'i is not ideal but this can be resolved by introducing Water. To diminish the power of Broken Fate, use Earth; the influence of Six Curses can be reduced with the addition of Wood. Accidents and Five Ghosts are in your element, and as a result it is difficult to offer further general advice.

HOUSE FACING NORTH		
Sheng ch'i Source of ch'i	Nien yen Long life	Chueh ming Broken fate
T'ien I Heavenly doctor		Hai huo Accidents
Wu kuei Five ghosts	Fu wei Bowing to the throne ↓ North	Liu sha Six curses

Source of Ch'i and Heavenly Doctor are both in your element; activate them further with Water. Long Life is not as well placed, but the use of Wood will support you. Accidents and Six Curses can both be neutralised by Water. Broken Fate and Five Ghosts are both in fairly favourable areas and cannot easily be improved.

HOUSE FACING NORTH-EAST		
Hai huo Accidents	Sheng ch'i Source of ch'i	Nien yen Long life
Chueh ming Broken fate		T'ien I Heavenly doctor
Liu sha Six curses	Fu wei Bowing to the throne ↓ North-east	Wu kuei Five ghosts

Source of Ch'i is reasonably well placed and difficult to improve. In order to utilise Long Life and Heavenly Doctor, the influence of Water will be needed. Five Ghosts can be neutralised with Wood and Accidents tempered with Earth. Since Broken Fate and Six Curses are in your element, their negative influence is balanced out and it is difficult to improve them.

HOUSE FACING EAST		
Hai huo Accidents	*Chueh ming* Broken fate	*Wu kuei* Five ghosts
Sheng ch'i Source of ch'i		*T'ien I* Heavenly doctor
Nien yen Long life	*Fu wei* Bowing to the throne ↓ East	*Liu sha* Six curses

Heavenly Doctor is very well placed; support it further with additional Water. Long Life is also well placed and can be supported with Wood. Source of Ch'i is not ideal, but you can provide support with Wood. The influence of Broken Fate and Five Ghosts can be weakened by Water. The influence of Accidents and Six Curses is diminished, because they are both located within favourable areas and, as a result, it is difficult to improve this further.

HOUSE FACING SOUTH-EAST		
Liu sha Six curses	*Hai huo* Accidents	*Sheng ch'i* Source of ch'i
Wu kuei Five ghosts		*Chueh ming* Broken fate
T'ien I Heavenly doctor	*Fu wei* Bowing to the throne ↓ South-east	*Nien yen* Long life

Source of Ch'i is very well placed; use Wood to harness it further. Long Life is in your element, but you can support it with additional Wood. Heavenly Doctor is not ideal, so introduce Earth to make it more accessible. The influence of Accidents and Six Curses can both be diluted with the use of Water. The influences of Broken Fate and Five Ghosts are diminished, since they are in a favourable area.

Fire People at Home

風水

This chapter will show Fire people how to make the best use of the energies in the home.

Fire male

FIRE	SELF	FRIENDS	COMPETITORS
Earth	Expression	Career	Positive outlets
Metal	Wealth	Conquests	Spouse
Water	Pressure	Status	Children and father
Wood	Resources	Support	Mother

Fire female

FIRE	SELF	FRIENDS	COMPETITORS
Earth	Children	Career	Positive outlets
Metal	Wealth	Conquests	Father
Water	Pressure	Status	Spouse
Wood	Resources	Support	Mother

As a Fire person, your wealth is represented by Metal, since Fire is said to control Metal. Your resources and support are associated with Wood, since Wood is said to generate Fire. Earth represents your career and the way you express yourself, since Fire creates Earth, and Water is associated with pressure, since Water is said to control Fire. When we are strong, we can handle pressure and so acquire status (see page 75).

HOUSE FACING SOUTH		
Chueh ming Broken fate	*Nien yen* Long life	*Hai huo* Accidents
Wu kuei Five ghosts		*Sheng ch'i* Source of ch'i
Liu sha Six curses	*Fu wei* Bowing to the throne ↓ South	*T'ien I* Heavenly doctor

Heavenly Doctor and Source of Ch'i are both ideally placed, although you can harness them further with Fire. Long Life is not ideally placed but Wood will improve this area for you. The influence of Accidents and Six Curses can be reduced by introducing Metal, and since Broken Fate and Five Ghosts are in a favourable area, their influence is already reduced and difficult to improve.

HOUSE FACING SOUTH-WEST		
Chueh ming Broken fate	*Sheng ch'i* Source of ch'i	*Hai huo* Accidents
Nien yen Long life		*Wu kuei* Five ghosts
T'ien I Heavenly doctor	*Fu wei* Bowing to the throne ↓ South-west	*Liu sha* Six curses

Heavenly Doctor and Long Life are reasonably placed and difficult to improve. Although Source of Ch'i is not ideal, introducing Fire will make it more favourable. Broken Fate can be minimised with Wood. Since Five Ghosts, Accidents and Six Curses are in all in favourable positions, it is difficult to improve on these.

HOUSE FACING WEST		
Nien yen Long life	Chueh ming Broken fate	Liu sha Six curses
Hai huo Accidents		Wu kuei Five ghosts
Sheng ch'i Source of ch'i	Fu wei Bowing to the throne ↓ West	T'ien I Heavenly doctor

Source of Ch'i is reasonably placed and difficult to improve. Long Life and Heavenly Doctor will both need the support of Fire. Broken Fate and Six Curses will also benefit from Fire, and the area associated with Accidents can be neutralised by Wood. Since Five Ghosts is in a favourable area, negativity is reduced and it is difficult to improve this.

HOUSE FACING NORTH-WEST		
Wu kuei Five ghosts	Hai huo Accidents	Chueh ming Broken fate
T'ien I Heavenly doctor		Nien yen Long life
Liu sha Six curses	Fu wei Bowing to the throne ↓ North-west	Sheng ch'i Source of ch'i

Source of Ch'i is reasonably placed and difficult to improve. Long Life and Heavenly Doctor will both need the support of Fire. Introduce Wood to reduce the influence of Six Curses, and to weaken Five Ghosts and Accidents, introduce Fire. The area associated with Broken Fate is in a favourable position and again it would be difficult to improve this.

HOUSE FACING NORTH		
Sheng ch'i Source of ch'i	Nien yen Long life	Chueh ming Broken fate
T'ien I Heavenly doctor		Hai huo Accidents
Wu kuei Five ghosts	Fu wei Bowing to the throne ↓ North	Liu sha Six curses

Source of Ch'i and Heavenly Doctor are located in very auspicious areas but you can introduce Fire to harness them even more. Long Life is also favourable and would benefit further with additional Wood. The influence of Broken Fate and Five Ghosts can be diluted with Metal. Since Accidents and Six Curses are well placed, these are difficult to improve.

HOUSE FACING NORTH-EAST		
Hai huo Accidents	Sheng ch'i Source of ch'i	Nien yen Long life
Chueh ming Broken fate		T'ien I Heavenly doctor
Liu sha Six curses	Fu wei Bowing to the throne ↓ North-east	Wu kuei Five ghosts

Heavenly Doctor and Long Life are reasonably placed and difficult to improve. Source of Ch'i is not ideal, but introducing Fire will support you further. Broken Fate and Six Curses are in favourable areas; introduce Fire to improve them further. Introduce Wood to neutralise Five Ghosts; since Accidents are in a favourable area, this is difficult to improve.

HOUSE FACING EAST		
Hai huo Accidents	*Chueh ming* Broken fate	*Wu kuei* Five ghosts
Sheng ch'i Source of ch'i		*T'ien I* Heavenly doctor
Nien yen Long life	*Fu wei* Bowing to the throne ↓ East	*Liu sha* Six curses

Long Life is ideally placed; introduce Wood to support it further. Source of Ch'i is also excellent but you can improve this with Fire. Heavenly Doctor is not well placed, and you will need Wood in order to utilise this area. The influence of Accidents and Six Curses can be minimised by the use of Metal. Broken Fate and Five Ghosts are in favourable areas, so are difficult to improve.

HOUSE FACING SOUTH-EAST		
Liu sha Six curses	*Hai huo* Accidents	*Sheng ch'i* Source of ch'i
Wu kuei Five ghosts		*Chueh ming* Broken fate
T'ien I Heavenly doctor	*Fu wei* Bowing to the throne ↓ South-east	*Nien yen* Long life

Long Life is ideally placed; harness it further with Fire. Heavenly Doctor is also well placed but can be supported with additional Wood. Source of Ch'i is not in the ideal position, but this can be remedied by the introduction of Wood. The influence of Broken Fate and Five Ghosts can be diluted with Metal. Accidents and Six Curses are in favourable areas and so are difficult to improve.

Earth People at Home

風水

This chapter will show Earth people how to make the best use of the energies in the home.

Fire male

EARTH	SELF	FRIENDS	COMPETITORS
Metal	Expression	Career	Positive outlets
Water	Wealth	Conquests	Spouse
Wood	Pressure	Status	Children and father
Fire	Resources	Support	Mother

Fire female

EARTH	SELF	FRIENDS	COMPETITORS
Metal	Children	Career	Positive outlets
Water	Wealth	Conquests	Father
Wood	Pressure	Status	Spouse
Fire	Resources	Support	Mother

As an Earth person, your wealth is represented by Water, since Earth is said to control Water. Your resources and support are associated with Fire, since Fire is said to generate Earth. Metal represents your career and the way you express yourself, since Earth creates Metal, and Wood is associated with pressure, since Wood is said to control Earth. When we are strong, we can cope with pressure; when this happens, we acquire status (see page 75).

HOUSE FACING SOUTH		
Chueh ming Broken fate	Nien yen Long life	Hai huo Accidents
Wu kuei Five ghosts		Sheng ch'i Source of ch'i
Liu sha Six curses	Fu wei Bowing to the throne	T'ien I Heavenly doctor

South ↓

Long Life is fairly favourable and difficult to improve. To utilise Heavenly Doctor and Source of Ch'i, the influence of Fire will be needed on both. To reduce the effects of Broken Fate and Five Ghosts, introduce the Water element. Since Accidents and Six Curses are both in your element, it is difficult to advise additional improvements.

HOUSE FACING SOUTH-WEST		
Chueh ming Broken fate	Sheng ch'i Source of ch'i	Hai huo Accidents
Nien yen Long life		Wu kuei Five ghosts
T'ien I Heavenly doctor	Fu wei Bowing to the throne	Liu sha Six curses

South-west ↓

Source of Ch'i is ideally placed but can be supported further with additional Earth. In order to utilise Long Life and Heavenly Doctor, the support of Earth will also be needed. Fire is needed to neutralise the effects of Five Ghosts and Accidents. Add the Earth element to improve Six Curses. Broken Fate is in a fairly favourable position and difficult to improve.

HOUSE FACING WEST		
Nien yen Long life	*Chueh ming* Broken fate	*Liu sha* Six curses
Hai huo Accidents		*Wu kuei* Five ghosts
Sheng ch'i Source of ch'i	*Fu wei* Bowing to the throne ↓ West	*T'ien I* Heavenly doctor

Long Life and Heavenly Doctor are both in your element but Fire will offer additional support. In order to utilise the Source of Ch'i, introduce Earth. Broken Fate and Six Curses can be tamed by the use of Fire, and Five Ghosts controlled by the use of Earth. The influence of Accidents is reduced because it is in a favourable area and is difficult to improve.

HOUSE FACING NORTH-WEST		
Wu kuei Five ghosts	*Hai huo* Accidents	*Chueh ming* Broken fate
T'ien I Heavenly doctor		*Nien yen* Long life
Liu sha Six curses	*Fu wei* Bowing to the throne ↓ North-west	*Sheng ch'i* Source of ch'i

Heavenly Doctor and Long Life are both in your element and can be supported with additional Earth. Source of Ch'i is not ideal, but this can again be supported with Earth. Five Ghosts and Accidents can both be depleted with Fire and Broken Fate with Earth. The influence of Six Curses is reduced by its position in a favourable element and is therefore difficult to improve.

HOUSE FACING NORTH		
Sheng ch'i Source of ch'i	Nien yen Long life	Chueh ming Broken fate
T'ien I Heavenly doctor		Hai huo Accidents
Wu kuei Five ghosts	Fu wei Bowing to the throne ↓ North	Liu sha Six curses

Long Life is ideally placed; harness it further with Earth. To utilise Heavenly Doctor and Source of Ch'i, these will both need the influence of Fire. Broken Fate and Five Ghosts are both in your element, their negative influence is already weakened and it is difficult to improve the situation. Accidents and Six Curses can be diluted by the addition of the Water element.

HOUSE FACING NORTH-EAST		
Hai huo Accidents	Sheng ch'i Source of ch'i	Nien yen Long life
Chueh ming Broken fate		T'ien I Heavenly doctor
Liu sha Six curses	Fu wei Bowing to the throne ↓ North-east	Wu kuei Five ghosts

Source of Ch'i is well placed and can be enhanced with additional Fire. Long Life and Heavenly Doctor are not in ideal locations, but introducing Earth will remedy this. Accidents can be neutralised with Earth; Broken Fate and Six Curses will both need the support of Fire. The influence of Five Ghosts is already reduced because of its favourable element and is therefore difficult to improve.

HOUSE FACING EAST		
Hai huo Accidents	*Chueh ming* Broken fate	*Wu kuei* Five ghosts
Sheng ch'i Source of ch'i		*T'ien I* Heavenly doctor
Nien yen Long life	*Fu wei* Bowing to the throne ↓ East	*Liu sha* Six curses

Source of Ch'i is very well placed: use Earth to harness it further. Heavenly Doctor is also quite well placed and difficult to improve. Fire will be needed to utilise Long Life, and to minimise Broken Fate and Five Ghosts, introduce the Water element. Accidents and Six Curses are both in favourable areas and are difficult to improve further.

HOUSE FACING SOUTH-EAST		
Liu sha Six curses	*Hai huo* Accidents	*Sheng ch'i* Source of ch'i
Wu kuei Five ghosts		*Chueh ming* Broken fate
T'ien I Heavenly doctor	*Fu wei* Bowing to the throne ↓ South-east	*Nien yen* Long life

Heavenly Doctor is very well placed but, to enhance it further, support with Fire. Source of Ch'i is fairly favourable but can be improved with additional Water. You will need the influence of Fire to utilise Long Life. Water can be used to weaken Six Curses and Accidents. Since Broken Fate and Five Ghosts are both in your element, these are difficult to improve.

Metal People at Home

風水

This chapter will show Metal people how to make the best use of the energies in the home.

Metal male

METAL	SELF	FRIENDS	COMPETITORS
Water	Expression	Career	Positive outlets
Wood	Wealth	Conquests	Spouse
Fire	Pressure	Status	Children and father
Earth	Resources	Support	Mother

Metal female

METAL	SELF	FRIENDS	COMPETITORS
Water	Children	Career	Positive outlets
Wood	Wealth	Conquests	Father
Fire	Pressure	Status	Spouse
Earth	Resources	Support	Mother

As a Metal person, your wealth is represented by Wood, since Metal is said to control Wood. Your resources and support are associated with Earth, since Earth is said to generate Metal. Water represents your career and the way you express yourself, since Metal creates Water, and Fire is associated with pressure, since Fire is said to control Metal. When we are strong, we can cope with pressure; when this happens, we acquire status (see page 75).

HOUSE FACING SOUTH		
Chueh ming Broken fate	Nien yen Long life	Hai huo Accidents
Wu kuei Five ghosts		Sheng ch'i Source of ch'i
Liu sha Six curses	Fu wei Bowing to the throne ↓ South	T'ien I Heavenly doctor

Source of Ch'i and Heavenly Doctor are reasonably placed and difficult to improve. Long Life needs the support of Metal. Accidents and Six Curses are favourably placed but introducing Metal will help to reduce the negative aspects even further. Broken Fate and Five Ghosts are both in favourable areas, which helps to reduce their negative influences and so are difficult to improve.

HOUSE FACING SOUTH-WEST		
Chueh ming Broken fate	Sheng ch'i Source of ch'i	Hai huo Accidents
Nien yen Long life		Wu kuei Five ghosts
T'ien I Heavenly doctor	Fu wei Bowing to the throne ↓ South-west	Liu sha Six curses

Source of Ch'i is ideally placed; to harness it further, add Metal. Heavenly Doctor and Long Life are in your element, which is positive, but you can offer additional Earth for support. Broken Fate can be diminished with Wood, and Six Curses neutralised with Earth. Five Ghosts and Accidents are in favourable areas, reducing their negative aspects, and would be difficult to improve.

HOUSE FACING WEST		
Nien yen Long life	*Chueh ming* Broken fate	*Liu sha* Six curses
Hai huo Accidents		*Wu kuei* Five ghosts
Sheng ch'i Source of ch'i	*Fu wei* Bowing to the throne ↓ West	*T'ien I* Heavenly doctor

Source of Ch'i is in your element but additional Earth will enhance it. Long Life and Heavenly Doctor are also well placed but would benefit further with the addition of Metal. Five Ghosts can be neutralised with Earth, and Accidents diminished with Wood. Broken Fate and Six Curses are in favourable areas, reducing their negative effects, and it is difficult to improve them.

HOUSE FACING NORTH-WEST		
Wu kuei Five ghosts	*Hai huo* Accidents	*Chueh ming* Broken fate
T'ien I Heavenly doctor		*Nien yen* Long life
Liu sha Six curses	*Fu wei* Bowing to the throne ↓ North-west	*Sheng ch'i* Source of ch'i

Source of Ch'i is in your element but enhance this further with Earth. Long Life and Heavenly Doctor are also well placed; harness their influences even more with Metal. Six Curses can be diminished with Wood and the influence of Broken Fate can weakened by Earth. Accidents and Five Ghosts are already in favourable areas and are difficult to improve.

HOUSE FACING NORTH		
Sheng ch'i Source of ch'i	Nien yen Long life	Chueh ming Broken fate
T'ien I Heavenly doctor		Hai huo Accidents
Wu kuei Five ghosts	Fu wei Bowing to the throne ↓ North	Liu sha Six curses

Source of Ch'i and Heavenly Doctor are reasonably placed and difficult to improve. Introduce the Earth element to utilise Long Life. To weaken the effects of Broken Fate and Five Ghosts, introduce the Metal element. Accidents and Six Curses are in favourable areas for you, helping to neutralise their negativity, and it would be hard to improve on this.

HOUSE FACING NORTH-EAST		
Hai huo Accidents	Sheng ch'i Source of ch'i	Nien yen Long life
Chueh ming Broken fate		T'ien I Heavenly doctor
Liu sha Six curses	Fu wei Bowing to the throne ↓ North-east	Wu kuei Five ghosts

Source of Ch'i is ideally placed; introduce Metal to harness it even further. Long Life and Heavenly Doctor are in your element but can be supported further with additional Earth. Introduce the Earth element to diminish the effects of Accidents, and introduce Wood to dilute the influence of Five Ghosts. Broken Fate and Six Curses are both in favourable areas for you, which helps to reduce their negative effects.

HOUSE FACING EAST		
Hai huo Accidents	*Chueh ming* Broken fate	*Wu kuei* Five ghosts
Sheng ch'i Source of ch'i		*T'ien I* Heavenly doctor
Nien yen Long life	*Fu wei* Bowing to the throne	*Liu sha* Six curses

East ↓

Source of Ch'i is badly placed and needs to be improved with the addition of the Earth element. Heavenly Doctor is also not ideal and requires Wood to become useful. Long Life is fairly favourable and difficult to improve. Although Accidents and Six Curses are well placed, reduce their negative aspects further with Metal. Broken Fate and Five Ghosts are also well placed.

HOUSE FACING SOUTH-EAST		
Liu sha Six curses	*Hai huo* Accidents	*Sheng ch'i* Source of ch'i
Wu kuei Five ghosts		*Chueh ming* Broken fate
T'ien I Heavenly doctor	*Fu wei* Bowing to the throne	*Nien yen* Long life

South-east ↓

Source of Ch'i is badly placed, so introduce Metal to improve the energies. Long Life is reasonably well placed and difficult to improve. Heavenly Doctor is not ideal but Earth will make it accessible. Broken Fate and Five Ghosts are situated in favourable areas but you can weaken their negative aspects further with Metal. Accidents and Six Curses are in favourable areas and difficult to improve.

Personal Feng Shui for Business

風水

The following chapters develop the earlier examination of the portents and how they relate to the prosperity of your workplace, by using your personal element in relation to the energies of your business or workplace.

In each of the following sections, I have included all eight houses, so whatever your element and whatever direction your premises or office may face, you will find information relating to you and your business. Although it cannot be totally comprehensive, it will give you the basic information you need, by identifying the major aspects which influence your work.

Keep in mind the fact that the key is to bring the elements associated with the building, the business and yourself into harmony, while utilising the various aspects of change associated with each area.

Water People at Work

風水

This chapter shows Water people how to harmonise their personal energies with those at their workplace.

Water male

WATER	SELF	FRIENDS	COMPETITORS
Wood	Expression	Career	Positive outlets
Fire	Wealth	Conquests	Spouse
Earth	Pressure	Status	Children and father
Metal	Resources	Support	Mother

Water female

WATER	SELF	FRIENDS	COMPETITORS
Wood	Children	Career	Positive outlets
Fire	Wealth	Conquests	Father
Earth	Pressure	Status	Spouse
Metal	Resources	Support	Mother

The charts above imitate the way the five elements work. For you, as a Water person, Fire represents your wealth, since Water is said to control Fire. Your resources and support are associated with Metal, since Metal is said to generate Water. Wood represents your career and the way you express yourself, since Water creates Wood, and Earth represents pressure, since Earth is said to control Water. When our personal elements are strong, and we are under the influence of favourable elements, we can overcome problems more easily. In coping with adversity, we not only become stronger but also acquire credibility, acknowledgement and respect and thus greater status. As the proverb says, 'The measure of success is how well you fare in bad times'.

Your career or business may not always be associated with the Wood element, which represents your career, and it is important to identify the element that is associated with your profession because if you are in an occupation that is associated with the Earth element, then your personal element will need to be strengthened.

Premises Facing South – Fire Element

Businesses associated with Fire or Earth are ideally placed in south-facing premises, although if your business is Earth, as a Water person you will need to utilise the areas of the premises associated with Metal or Water, or run the risk of finding that your work is controlling you, rather than you being in control of your business. Water activities are also fairly favourable in premises facing south.

Metal activities are not well starred in this location and may not thrive, but the introduction of the Earth element will help to restore the prosperity of the business. If you need to do this, however, you should try to utilise the areas that support you, such as Metal and Water, or you may find that the business itself is doing well but at the expense of your own peace of mind. If your business belongs to the Wood element, further Wood will be needed to prevent the site draining the energies of the business and preventing work from going as well as it should.

Premises Facing South-west and North-east – Earth Element

Activities involving the elements Earth and Metal are well favoured here, but if your business belongs to the Earth element, then you will need to utilise your auspicious areas, or run the risk of being dominated by the business and the premises. If your occupation relates to the Wood element, it is also reasonably placed in premises facing south-west or north-east.

A Water business would be considered under threat in these locations, but the introduction of the Metal element would restore harmony, happiness and prosperity in your career. If the work is associated with the Fire element, you will need to support it with Wood. If this is the case, once again you have to utilise your favourable areas, like Metal and Water, or you may find that although the business prospers, you yourself will not feel happy and fulfilled in your job.

Premises Facing West and North-west – Metal Element

Metal and Water businesses should prosper here, and a Water person even more so, since both will be favourably influenced by the Metal element. Fire activities are also quite well placed in premises relating to Metal.

Wood activities are under threat in these locations and may therefore find it hard to be successful. However, the introduction of the Water element would transform the conflict into harmony, both boosting you as a Water person and also encouraging the business in which you are engaged to be successful. If your job relates to the Earth element, however, the energies of the business are in danger of being depleted by these sites. To balance this, introduce Fire to enhance the business, and try to locate your office in an area associated with either Metal or Water in order to ensure that your personal element remains strong and you are therefore able to work to your maximum capacity.

Premises Facing North – Water Element

Activities associated with Water and Wood both prosper here, but Water people in jobs that relate to Wood should try to strengthen their personal element by working primarily in areas associated with either Metal or Water. If this is not possible, they may find themselves low on energy and drive at work, so they would need to strengthen or support their personal element. An Earth business is reasonably favourable in a north-facing building, but again you would benefit from the support of the Metal areas to avoid feeling a sense of pressure or even threat.

Fire activities are under threat in this location, but this can be resolved with the use of Wood. However, as a Water Person, you will need to utilise the Metal and Water areas of the premises if you are to perform at your best. A Metal business is in danger of being depleted in this location and you may find that it lacks drive and purpose. The introduction of additional Metal will help to support both you personally and your success in your job.

Premises Facing South-east and East – Wood Element

Wood and Fire activities both flourish in premises facing south-east and east, although if you are a Water person and your business relates to Wood, you are in danger of feeling personally weakened. Avoid this by working as much as possible in areas associated with either Metal or Water. A Metal business is also reasonably favourable here.

These sites would be a threat to an Earth business but the use of Fire will help to restore prosperity to the business and make things run more smoothly. Since you are a Water person, however, you may find that this will direct any conflict at you, so you will need to utilise the areas associated with Metal and Water in order to enjoy the benefits.

If your work relates to the Water element, additional Water will be needed to support you and improve the potential for success of the business.

Wood People at Work

風水

This chapter gives all the information necessary for Wood people to harmonise their energies with those at work.

Wood male

WOOD	SELF	FRIENDS	COMPETITORS
Fire	Expression	Career	Positive outlets
Earth	Wealth	Conquests	Spouse
Metal	Pressure	Status	Children and father
Water	Resources	Support	Mother

Wood female

WOOD	SELF	FRIENDS	COMPETITORS
Fire	Children	Career	Positive outlets
Earth	Wealth	Conquests	Father
Metal	Pressure	Status	Spouse
Water	Resources	Support	Mother

For you, as a Wood person, Earth represents your wealth, since Wood is said to control Earth. Your resources and support are associated with Water, since Water is said to generate Wood. Fire represents your career and the way you express yourself, since Wood creates Fire. Metal is associated with pressure, since Metal is said to control Wood. When we are strong, we can handle pressure; when this happens, we acquire status (see page 101).

Your career or business may not always be associated with the Fire element, which represents your career, and it is important to identify the element that is associated with your profession because if you are in an occupation which is associated with the Metal element, then your personal element will need to be strengthened.

Premises Facing South – Fire Element

These premises are ideal for activities associated with the Fire and Earth elements, although as a Wood Person you will need to ensure that your desk or working space is in either a Water or a Wood area, otherwise you may find that your personal energy is sapped. If the element of the business is Water, this would be favourable for you, since the type of work done controls the premises, but also generates your personal energies.

If the business is associated with the Metal element, the introduction of Earth will help to boost the business, but if the business is Wood, you would need to introduce more Wood to prevent the energy influences of the premises draining away the energy of the business and making it less successful than it could be.

Premises Facing South-west and North-east – Earth Element

These directions are associated with the Earth element, which represents your wealth, and, if your business belongs to either Earth or Metal, this is very favourable. As a Wood person, you should try to work mainly in either a Water or Wood area of the building in order to maintain the strength of your personal element. If your business relates to Wood, this site is also favourable.

If you are working in a Water business in premises facing south-west or north-east, you will need to introduce Metal to absorb any excessive Earth energies and regenerate the business. Again, it would be beneficial if you could work in a Water or Wood area. If your business is associated with the Fire element, there is a danger that it will over-strengthen the influence of the premises and it would be a good idea to add the support of Wood so that the work proceeds in the best possible atmosphere.

Premises Facing West and North-west – Metal Element

Premises facing west and north-west are both ideal for activities associated with Metal and Water, although if your business is a Metal one you would be best to try to work mainly in a Water or Wood area within the building in order to help counterbalance the pressure of Metal on your personal energies. A Fire activity in these locations would be fairly favourable and would benefit from additional Wood.

If the business is associated with the Wood element, there may be a conflict with Metal. To overcome this, you would need to introduce Water to boost the business and also to provide support for you. If your occupation belongs to the Earth element, allow the energies of the premises to support and encourage the success of the business and concentrate on increasing the Water element to boost your personal fortunes.

Premises Facing North – Water Element

Because Water represents resources and support, this direction is very favourable, especially if your business belongs to either the Water or Wood element, since Water will support you both. If your business belongs to the Metal element, which denotes status and power to a Wood Person, these premises would help to support you. If your business belongs to the Earth element, this is also favourable.

A Fire-related occupation is less favourably placed in north-facing premises, but you can improve the situation by introducing additional Wood as this will encourage the element of the premises to feed the element of the business and at the same time will prevent the strength of the business element from draining your personal energy.

Premises Facing South-east and East – Wood Element

Since these directions are both associated with the Wood element, they provide an ideal location for either a Wood or Fire business.

If your business belongs to the Earth element, the introduction of the Fire element will help to boost the success of the business, but if the business is associated with the Metal element, the introduction of Water will help to improve the relationship between the premises and the business. A Water business in these locations is not ideal, but at least you are in harmony with the premises, which is certain to be beneficial.

Fire People at Work

風水

ire people should use this chapter to harmonise their personal and workplace elements.

Fire male

FIRE	SELF	FRIENDS	COMPETITORS
Earth	Expression	Career	Positive outlets
Metal	Wealth	Conquests	Spouse
Water	Pressure	Status	Children and father
Wood	Resources	Support	Mother

Fire female

FIRE	SELF	FRIENDS	COMPETITORS
Earth	Children	Career	Positive outlets
Metal	Wealth	Conquests	Father
Water	Pressure	Status	Spouse
Wood	Resources	Support	Mother

For you, a Fire person, Metal represents your wealth, since Fire is said to control Metal. Your resources and support are associated with Wood, since Wood is said to generate Fire. Earth represents your career and the way you express yourself, since Fire creates Earth, and Water is associated with pressure, since Water is said to control Fire. When we are strong, we can handle pressure; when this happens, we acquire status (see page 101).

Your career or business may not always be associated with the Earth element, which represents your career, and it is important to identify the element that is associated with your profession because, if you are in an occupation which is associated with the Water element, then your personal element will need to be strengthened.

Premises Facing South – Fire Element

This is a perfect site for either a Fire or Earth business, and for a Fire Person this site will bring additional benefits.

This site would not be beneficial to a Metal business, but the introduction of the Earth element would help to bring about harmony as well as strengthening the business. If the business activity belongs to the Wood element, additional Wood would help prevent the business from becoming depleted and therefore lacking the energy to succeed. The use of Water may help to stimulate the business, but this would put additional pressure on you, which may not be beneficial. If the occupation is related to Water, you should try to position yourself in a Wood or Fire area in order to ensure that you work at your optimum capability.

Premises Facing South-west and North-east – Earth Element

Businesses that are associated with Earth and Metal are ideally placed here, but as a Fire Person you should try to work mainly in an area associated with either Wood or Fire in order to maintain the strength of your personal element and therefore work at your best. Activities associated with the Wood element are also reasonably placed in premises facing south-west or north-east.

A Water business in these locations would benefit from the introduction of the Metal element, although again you should try to work primarily within a Wood or Fire area. If your business belongs to the Fire element, try to introduce Wood to prevent the site from draining energy and drive from both the business and you.

Premises Facing West and North-west – Metal Element

Activities associated with the Metal and Water elements are all very favourable here, although a Fire Person working in a job related to Water should try to work as much as possible in an area of the premises related to Wood or Fire in order to avoid finding their work exerts too much pressure on them and becomes stressful. If your business belongs to the Fire element, this is also fairly beneficial.

These locations are not really suitable for a Wood business, but the addition of the Water element would help to restore the balance, although you should try to position yourself in a Wood area. If your business belongs to the Earth element, the introduction of Fire will help to prevent the energies of the site from draining the potential success of the business.

Premises Facing North – Water Element

Activities associated with Wood or Water would naturally benefit from a north-facing location, although a Fire Person working in a job related to the Water element would need to spend as much as possible of their working time in an area associated with Wood or Fire in order to avoid feeling under constant pressure. This site is also suitable for Earth-related occupations.

A Fire business in this position would be under attack from the premises, creating a situation where the business would not flourish as it should. The introduction of the Wood element would help to boost not only the business but also your personal energies. If your job is associated with the Metal element, you will need to introduce Earth to prevent the site holding back the success of the business. You should also try to work as much as possible in a Wood area to keep your personal element strong.

Premises Facing South-east and East – Wood Element

Wood and Fire businesses both benefit from the influence of Wood, and for a Fire person these make ideal locations for your office or place of work. If your business belongs to the Earth element, the introduction of Fire will improve the balance of energies between the site and the activity, thus boosting the business. A Metal activity in these positions is reasonably favourable, since, as a Fire Person, you would control the business although the business controls the site. Additional Wood would help to support you even further.

If your business is associated with the Water element, introduce the Metal element but try to position yourself in a Wood or Fire area, otherwise you may find that you are not functioning efficiently.

Earth People at Work

風水

This chapter shows how Earth people can maximise their harmony with the elements at work.

Earth male

EARTH	SELF	FRIENDS	COMPETITORS
Metal	Expression	Career	Positive outlets
Water	Wealth	Conquests	Spouse
Wood	Pressure	Status	Children and father
Fire	Resources	Support	Mother

Earth female

EARTH	SELF	FRIENDS	COMPETITORS
Metal	Children	Career	Positive outlets
Water	Wealth	Conquests	Father
Wood	Pressure	Status	Spouse
Fire	Resources	Support	Mother

For you, an Earth person, Water represents your wealth, since Earth is said to control Water. Your resources and support are associated with Fire, since Fire is said to generate Earth. Metal represents your career and the way you express yourself, since Earth creates Metal, and Wood is associated with pressure, since Wood is said to control Earth.

Your career or business may not always be associated with the Metal element, which represents your career, and it is important to identify the element that is associated with your profession because, if you are in an occupation which is associated with the Wood element, then your personal element will need to be strengthened.

Premises Facing South – Fire Element

Obviously, activities that are associated with Fire and Earth will all benefit from being located in south-facing premises, and this would offer additional benefits to you, an Earth person. A Water activity is also reasonably favourable for this location.

This site would be most inauspicious for a Metal-related business, but the introduction of the Earth element would improve harmony and prosperity, not only for the business but also for you. A Wood business may be in danger of being drained by the site, resulting in the people having to work even harder for a limited degree of success, but additional Wood would balance this negative energy flow. However, you would then need to locate your desk, office or workplace in a Fire or Earth area if you want to work confidently and efficiently.

Premises Facing South-west and North-east – Earth Element

Businesses associated with either Earth or Metal are very favourable for sites facing south-west and north-east, especially for an Earth person. A Wood activity here is also fairly favourable.

If the occupation is associated with Water, then it may well be under threat here, but the introduction of the Metal element will help to restore the balance and ensure that work is creative and productive. If the business belongs to the Fire element, it will need the support of additional Wood to prevent it from being drained and constantly held back. Having added Wood, an Earth Person would be most successful working in an area of the building associated with either Fire or Earth.

Premises Facing West and North-west – Metal Element

Activities that are associated with either Metal or Water will all benefit from these sites, although Earth people working in a business belonging to the Metal element may find that they are lacking in personal energy and would feel best if they were working in areas of the building associated with either Fire or Earth. Activities associated with the Fire element are also reasonably placed here.

A Wood business in these locations is under threat from the strong energies of the site and is unlikely to thrive. However, the addition of the Water element will help to restore balance and harmony. If the business belongs to the Earth element, you will need to introduce Fire to prevent the conflicting energies of the site from draining the success of the business.

Premises facing North – Water Element

Activities associated with either Water or Wood are very favourable in north-facing premises, although Earth people working in a job related to Wood would need to concentrate their time in an area associated with either Fire or Earth to avoid feeling under extreme pressure. An Earth business is also quite favourable in north-facing premises.

A Fire business would be inauspicious here and would therefore find more than the usual number of obstacles in its path, but the introduction of the

Wood element would boost the business by restoring the balance. However, Earth people might find themselves lacking in energy unless they were working in an area associated with Fire or Earth. If the occupation is associated with the Metal element, you will need to introduce additional Earth to prevent the energies of the site from draining the potential for success of the business.

Premises Facing South-east and East – Wood Element

Businesses associated with either Wood or Fire are well placed here, although if the work is Wood-related, you will need to position yourself in an area associated with Fire or Earth in order to work to your optimum capacity. A Fire business should thrive here and any additional Fire will not only boost the business but also help to support you.

Activities associated with the Earth element would be under threat in premises facing south-east or east but, again, the use of Fire would bring harmony and prosperity to both you personally and the business. Water activities are in danger of being drained by the site and would need the support of Metal, but if this is the case, be careful to make use of Fire to prevent your personal energies from being drained away and to ensure that you can work as effectively as you should.

Metal People at Work

風水

etal people can follow this information for maximum harmony at work.

Metal male

METAL:	SELF	FRIENDS	COMPETITORS
Water	Expression	Career	Positive outlets
Wood	Wealth	Conquests	Spouse
Fire	Pressure	Status	Children and father
Earth	Resources	Support	Mother

Metal female

METAL	SELF	FRIENDS	COMPETITORS
Water	Children	Career	Positive outlets
Wood	Wealth	Conquests	Father
Fire	Pressure	Status	Spouse
Earth	Resources	Support	Mother

As a Metal person, Wood represents your wealth, since Metal is said to control Wood. Your resources and support are associated with Earth, since Earth is said to generate Metal. Water represents your career and the way you express yourself, since Metal creates Water, and Fire is associated with pressure, since Fire is said to control Metal.

Your career or business may not always be associated with the Water element, which represents your career, and if you are in an occupation that is associated with the Fire element, then your personal element will need to be strengthened.

Premises Facing South – Fire Element

Occupations associated with Fire and Earth both prosper in south-facing premises, but as a Metal person working in a Fire-related occupation, you should try to spend most of your time in an area that offers personal support, such as Earth or Metal, in order to work at your best. In the case of a Water activity, this site is also fairly favourable.

A Metal business would be under attack in this location, but this can be resolved with the use of Earth, which would both boost your personal energy and also encourage the business to succeed. If the business belongs to the Wood element, the influence of Water will be necessary to prevent the site from draining the energies and, with them, the potential success of the business. If this is the case, position yourself in either an Earth or Metal area to avoid the risk of finding that you are lacking in personal energy.

Premises Facing South-west and North-east – Earth Element

Obviously, activities associated with either Earth or Metal should prosper here and if these represent your business you, as a Metal Person, would also benefit greatly. Wood activities are also reasonably favourable in premises facing south-west and north-east.

A Water business is not so fortunate, but the introduction of the Metal element would not only improve relations, but would also boost both your own energy and that of your business. If your occupation is associated with the Fire element, the introduction of the Wood element would help to prevent the site from draining the success of the business. If you do add Wood, make sure you spend as much as possible of your time in an area associated with Earth or Metal in order to avoid any personal conflict with your personal element of Metal. You will find that you work best in those areas.

Premises Facing West and North-west – Metal Element

Metal and Water activities both thrive in these locations, but if your business is associated with the Water element, you will need to position your desk or workplace within areas associated with Earth or Metal to prevent the strength of the business element from draining your own energies and making you feel listless and apathetic. Fire activities are reasonably placed in premises facing west and north-west, although it may be useful to utilise the Earth areas for personal support. If your business belongs to the Earth element, support it with additional Earth to prevent the site from draining the positive energies from the business.

A Wood business would not do well in these locations, but the introduction of the Water element would help to restore relations between the business and the site. However, in order to prevent you suffering as a result of this action, try to ensure that you spend most of your working time in areas associated with either Earth or Metal.

Premises Facing North – Water Element

Activities associated with Water and Wood are very favourable in north-facing premises but, if your business is Water, then you will need to position yourself in an area associated with either Earth or Metal, or run the risk of lacking energy for work. If the business belongs to the Earth element, this is also a fairly favourable site.

This site would be inauspicious for Fire activities, which are unlikely to thrive, but the introduction of the Wood element should restore balance and harmony, while helping to generate the business at the same time. A Metal business in this location is in danger of being depleted by the site. To help combat this, the introduction of additional Metal would help support both the business and your personal energy.

Premises Facing South-east and East – Wood Element

Businesses associated with either Wood or Fire are very favourable here, although a Metal Person working in a Fire occupation would do well to work in an area associated with either Earth or Metal to avoid feeling under constant pressure and becoming stressed. A Metal occupation is also reasonably placed here.

An Earth business is under threat here and the business may not be doing as well as it should. Introducing the Fire element would help to improve the balance of energies between the site and the business. However, in this case, you too will need the support of Fire or Earth to avoid being depleted yourself. If the business is related to Water, introduce additional Metal to boost yourself and to prevent the site from draining the positive energies from your business.

The House of Spouse

風水

Sometimes when we meet someone for the first time, we feel an instant attraction towards them that we, in the West, often describe as 'chemistry'. This is exactly how the Chinese view it, although they do not see it as something intangible and indefinable but as another aspect of the metaphysical principles that relate to all things from character to energy and fate. They see this 'chemistry' as something that can be identified and defined.

In Chinese terms, we are attracted to what we need, not necessarily in a physical, conscious way, but in a metaphysical sense. If we are lacking in certain elements, we are naturally attracted to people who possess those elements, and if they are attracted to us, it is because we have the elements that they need. To the Chinese, this is known as *yuen*, or metaphysical attraction. Very often, it can be heavenly, exhilarating and exciting, but without compatibility, it is often short and sweet. If a couple meet and discover that each was born on a day that supplies those elements missing in the other, this can cause a mutual attraction, which can often flourish and develop very quickly. This is the Chinese version of our idea that 'opposites attract'.

We all know of people who, for a variety of reasons, seem to establish relationships with the wrong sort of partners and who seem unable to change this or even explain why. Instant attraction and real compatibility, however, are very different things, and attraction alone is not enough in itself to sustain a long, happy and harmonious relationship.

For over 1,000 years, traditional Chinese families have used a unique system to help secure compatible, happy and harmonious marriages for their children, and the same practice is still in use by many families today.

Even before the business of courting can begin, each family carries out a thorough investigation of potential partners to determine whether they are a suitable match for the son or daughter of the family. This investigation is primarily based on the Pillars of Destiny, as defined in the ancient Chinese calendar and explained in previous chapters.

As far as the Chinese are concerned, these pillars represent a person's unique metaphysical signature and they offer valuable insights into each individual. They provide an indication of individual characteristics, needs and desires, as well as what each person finds attractive in others and what others are likely to find attractive in them.

If a man wants to express his romantic interest in a particular girl, he presents to her father a red card. On the card will be written his 'Eight Characters', information based on his Pillars of Destiny. This card is both symbolic of his intentions towards the girl, and also that he is asking to be seriously considered as a suitor. At the same time, he is given a red card marked with the girl's characters, so that his family can go through the same process on his behalf and ensure that the girl of his dreams is also compatible with him. Once both families have reassured themselves that there is potential in the relationship, the serious business of courtship can begin.

Instant attraction can be a very powerful force but without real compatibility any couple will find that their relationship will have much less chance of enduring. With the high and increasing rate of divorce and relationship failure and the wide-ranging negative impacts of break-ups on all concerned, the Chinese see it as logical to look for the best possible ways to secure sound, loving and long-lasting relationships.

The Branch of the Day Pillar

In Chinese terms, the House of Spouse represents the earthly branch of our day pillar, and by looking at this and comparing it with our own personal element, which is the stem of our day pillar, we can create an accurate picture both of the type of partner we attract and the type of partner we find attractive. This is because knowing the House of Spouse will tell us the relationship between the elements relating to us and our partner and therefore indicate whether we support, control, deplete or submit to our partner. This may or may not be beneficial, but it will explain why we are sometimes attracted to the wrong people and why relationships develop in certain ways. It is also very important to realise that although these diferent aspects of mutual attraction can be good both for ourselves and our partners, a relationship can only work if it suits both partners.

For example, a person whose element is yang Fire and who has yang Wood in their House of Spouse would be attracted to partners who generate and support them in elemental terms. If they find a partner who has a very strong Wood element in their make-up and is completely lacking in Fire, this relationship would work very well since both partners would be getting what they needed. However, if they attract a Wood partner whose element is weak, their need for support may well deplete the energies of their weak Wood partner; after all, Fire feeds on Wood.

Ideally, therefore, we should be able to consider all aspects of a person's make-up before we embark on a relationship. In practice, of course, life simply is not like that. When we meet someone for the first time, we make a decision there and then as to whether there is a mutual attraction. It is only later that we begin to consider the compatibility factor, by which time it may be too late, as even if we realise that the relationship is incompatible, we may already have fallen in love.

The only way to try to prevent this situation is to examine our own needs and attractions and to know as much as possible about ourselves in the first place. We can then get some idea of the type of relationship that suits us best, as well as those that would not suit us – even though they may initially be attractive. Subsequently, it is up to us to consider both the attraction and compatibility aspects of potential partners.

You will be able to use this book to establish your day pillar and the strength of your personal element so that you can then determine the favourable and unfavourable elements of your House of Spouse. Once you have determined from the tables the relevant factors relating to the day on which you were born, you can follow through to find out all about your House of Spouse. For example, if you were born on the day of the yang Metal Monkey, turn to the section for yang Metal people and then read the information which is given for those born on that day.

If you are single, unattached and hoping to meet your soul-mate, take a little time to investigate the day pillars and particularly the personal element of any potential partner, to see if they are compatible with you. This should give you some guidance on whether to pursue the relationship. If you are interested in more than one person, this may also help you to make the right choice.

Relationships for Yang Water People

風水

1 f you have determined that you are a yang Water person, this section will tell you more about your House of Spouse. Turn first to the section on pages 57–60, which defines the element and animal associated with your birth date. This is your House of Spouse.

Yang Water people often attract and are attracted to yin Fire people.

Born on the Day of the Water Rat

The Rat is associated with the Water element and for a Water person this indicates that you are attracted to those whom you identify as being similar to yourself.

This type of relationship can work very well, especially if you and your partner are both weak Water people, in which case you will support, nourish and rejuvenate each other. On the negative side, you may compete with each other in this relationship and if you are both strong Water people, this may lead to conflict. If you are a weak Water person, then you may well be attracted to Metal people, especially if you feel somewhat exhausted, because they will certainly help to put the smile back on your face. If your element is strong and you relish a challenge, then seek out the company of Earth people, who will provide a certain amount of provocation.

Born on the Day of the Water Tiger

Since the Tiger is associated with the Wood element, this suggests that you as a Water person like to support, encourage and pamper your partner. Another aspect of this combination is that you also have the ability to attract people who are seeking a partner who will do everything for them.

If your personal element is weak, this kind of relationship can leave you very vulnerable and completely exhausted, and in this case you may prefer the company of Metal people who will replenish your energy. However, if your element is strong and your partner thrives on this level of support, this combination can work very well. If you are a fairly dominant, strong Water person, you may well find that a Fire person is your ideal partner, as long as this also suits them; otherwise you run the risk of becoming over-domineering.

Born on the Day of the Water Dragon

The Dragon is associated with the Earth element, which offers quite a challenge for a Water person, as you may attract people who will tend to dominate you.

If your personal element is strong, however, this could provide the stimulation you need as long as your partner is happy to take control and their personal element is strong enough to face the challenge. If you are a weak Water person looking for an easy life, conflict and challenge may be the last thing you need, in which case perhaps you will find that your soulmate belongs to the Metal element, as they will provide you with all the love and care you crave. Perhaps you feel happiest when you are lavishing attention on your partner and, if this is the sort of relationship you are looking for, then a Wood person would be the right one for you, so long as they appreciate your support and encouragement.

Born on the Day of the Water Horse

Because the Horse is associated with the Fire element, as a Water person this House of Spouse suggests that you like to be in charge, at least as far as your relationships are concerned, and as a result you may also attract submissive partners.

This may not be the best combination, especially if their personal element is weak and yours is strong, because the chances are that you will tend to dominate your partner, which may have an adverse effect on them. If you are in this kind of relationship, try to exercise a little more restraint and allow your partner more space to grow, because even if your efforts are well intentioned, your partner may feel smothered by your attentions. If you are a strong Water person, you may relish the prospect of a more challenging relationship, in which case you should look for an Earth person as a partner.

Born on the Day of the Water Monkey

The element associated with the Monkey is Metal and since this generates Water, this House of Spouse suggests that you are attracted to people who can stimulate and inspire you, although you also run the risk of becoming dependent on your partner.

If your partner is a strong Metal person, they are unlikely to be affected by your demands, but if not, your energy may well deplete theirs, so try not to let this happen. If you are a strong Water person, support and encouragement may not be the qualities that you seek from your partner, preferring instead someone who is capable of providing you with a challenge in life. If this is you, then you should consider the company of an Earth person, who is more likely be able to provide this, or a Wood person, who would allow you the opportunity to shine and express yourself.

Born on the Day of the Water Dog

The Dog is associated with the Earth element and since this is said to control Water, there is a danger here that you will be dominated by your partner, especially if you are a weak Water person.

If this does not appeal to you, look to the charms of a Metal person, who would no doubt supply all the care and attention that you desire. If you are a strong Water person, you may thrive in a relationship in which your partner dominates, providing you with the challenge that you need in life, but if you are in love with the idea of lavishing your time and energy on your partner, then perhaps you should consider focusing your attention on a Wood person, who is more likely to be happy with the attention you can bestow on them.

Relationships for Yin Water People

風水

If you have determined that you are a yin Water person, this section will tell you more about your House of Spouse. Turn first to the section on pages 57–60, which defines the element and animal associated with your birth date. This is your House of Spouse.

Yin Water people often attract and are attracted to yang Earth people.

Born on the Day of the Water Ox

The Ox is associated with the Earth element, which can be a mixed blessing for a Water person. If you are a strong Water person, you probably attract powerful partners who provide you with status, but if you are a weak Water person, then you may attract partners who want to dominate you; if your personal element is weak, this may well have a debilitating effect on you.

As a strong Water person, you may prefer to take the lead in your relationships and so a Fire person may present an attractive proposition, but this will only work if they are in need of your Water; if not, things may not be as harmonious as you may imagine. If you enjoy spoiling and pampering your partner, then try a Wood person, but again, this will only work if they appreciate your level of support.

Born on the Day of the Water Rabbit

This House of Spouse denotes that you like to support and encourage your partner because the element of the Rabbit is Wood, which is fed and nurtured by Water. However, in some instances, Wood can also deplete Water.

If you are a weak Water person and your partner is a strong Wood person, then the best advice is to learn to say 'No', otherwise you will run the risk of exhausting yourself. If your element is weak and you dream of having a partner who will support and encourage you, then look no further than a Metal person, who is certain to have the capacity to rejuvenate and replenish you. If your element is strong, you may prefer a partner who offers you more of a challenge, such as an Earth person, or someone you could pamper, such as a Wood person.

Born on the Day of the Water Snake

The Snake is associated with the Fire element, indicating that you like to take the leading role in a relationship.

Although this may suit you, it may not suit your partner, especially if they are a weak Fire person. On the other hand, if their element is strong, then they may well prosper under your influence, guidance and control. If you are a weak Water person, taking control is the last thing on your mind and therefore you may prefer a partner who can take the lead in a relationship. If this is the case, you may well benefit from a partner belonging to the Metal element, who will provide you with all the love and care that you will need in order to flourish and prosper, since Metal generates Water.

Born on the Day of the Water Sheep

The Sheep is associated with the Earth element and, since this is said to control Water, this House of Spouse denotes that you attract dominant partners. This may or may not suit you, depending on the strength of your personal element.

Powerful and dominant people can be very attractive to some people, but if you are a weak Water person, the chances are that this type of relationship will have an adverse effect on you, leaving you feeling subdued rather than revitalised. If you are lacking a boost in life, seek out the company of Metal people, who have the ability to rejuvenate and replenish you, providing of course that their personal element is strong enough for the task and they are looking for someone to lavish their love and affection on.

Born on the Day of the Water Rooster

This House of Spouse may just provide you with all that you need, especially if you are a weak Water person, who thrives with loving support and encouragement from your partner. Of course, this will only work if your partner's element is strong enough to cope with your demands because, if not, you may only end up draining your partner, which would not benefit either of you.

If you are a strong Water person, support and encouragement may not be high on your agenda and, if this applies to you, then perhaps you would relish the sort of challenge that only an Earth person can provide. Alternatively, if you like to take the initiative in your relationships, then a Fire person may be your perfect match, but only if they are happy for you to be in control; otherwise it may well end up in tears for someone.

Born on the Day of the Water Pig

The Pig is associated with the Water element and for a Water person, this House of Spouse suggests that you attract and are attracted to people who are similar to yourself. This can be very harmonious, since it denotes that you will encourage and support each other, if you can avoid having to compete with each other.

While this may suit some people, there will be others who are looking for a bit more spice in their life. For those who like a challenge, then an Earth person may just fit the bill and for those who like to be in charge, then perhaps a Fire person would be more suitable. For those looking for a soul-mate who will stimulate and inspire them, then look no further than a Metal person, because they are certain to brighten up your life.

Relationships for Yang Wood People

風水

f you have determined that you are a yang Wood person, this section will tell you more about your House of Spouse. Turn first to the section on pages 57–60, which defines the element and animal associated with your birth date. This is your House of Spouse.

Yang Wood people can often attract and be attracted to yin Earth people.

Born on the Day of the Wood Rat

The Rat is associated with Water, which for a Wood person represents support, so you will attract and be attracted to people who can offer you support and encouragement.

If you are a weak Wood person, this will be even more significant and, as Wood also depletes Water, you should try not to become too dependent on your partner. If you have suffered in relationships where your partner has tried to restrict or control you, someone who regenerates and inspires you will obviously help you to flourish and prosper. If you are a strong Wood Person and are lacking in Fire, this type of relationship may not be ideal because instead of looking for support, you will be looking for outlets for your energies. In that case, a Fire person may be more suitable because they offer a positive outlet for the Wood element.

Born on the Day of the Wood Tiger

The Tiger is also associated with Wood, so you are attracted to partners who share a lot in common with you.

This can work well if you are a weak Wood person who would benefit from support, but if you are a strong Wood person, this can result in competition with your partner. If your partner is also a Wood person, you should try to give each other some space because otherwise you run the risk of smothering or competing with each other so that you end up bitter rivals instead of lovers. If you and your partner both need the support of Wood, then this is very good. As a strong Wood person, you may be attracted to Fire people, who would provide you with the perfect opportunity to express yourself fully, or Metal people who would provide you with a challenge.

Born on the Day of the Wood Dragon

The Dragon is associated with Earth and, since Wood is said to control Earth, you may attract a submissive partner.

This may work well for a strong Wood person, provided that their partner is happy, otherwise this will cause conflict. If you are a weak Wood person, having a partner who expects you to take charge all the time could leave you feeling drained. If you are a strong Wood person, you may prefer a partner you could lavish your attention on, in which case a Fire person may be ideal; but if it's a challenge you are looking for, go for a Metal partner. As a Wood person, Earth represents your wealth and to have your wealth in your House of Spouse can be a blessing, but it can also be a reminder not to place too much emphasis on financial considerations when selecting a partner. The Dragon is also known to store Water and this denotes that you may well receive more support than you realise.

Born on the Day of the Wood Horse

The Horse is associated with Fire and, since Wood feeds Fire, you are likely to be attracted to people you can nurture and nourish and you will be attracted to people who want to be supported.

A partner to care for may work when your personal element is strong, but when it is weak, your partner has the potential to deplete your energy and you may be better to team up with someone who can offer you support, rather than being expected to take the initiative all the time. If your element is strong and your partner is Fire, you should expect to support and nurture them – after all, as far as Fire is concerned, that is what Wood is for – but if your element is weak, you may be better suited to a Water person.

Born on the Day of the Wood Monkey

The Monkey is associated with the Metal element, which is said to control Wood, so this denotes that you may be attracted to dominant partners.

Of course, if this suits you both, then this does not present a problem, but if your Wood is weak, this may well have a debilitating effect on you. If you attract partners who wish to control you and your own element is weak, then the chances are that this type of relationship will not suit you. Try to avoid these and look instead for someone who will support you, like a Water person. A strong, determined, powerful partner can be very attractive for some people but you may well find others more appealing.

Born on the Day of the Wood Dog

The Dog is associated with the Earth element, which is said to be controlled by Wood, and this indicates that you may tend to dominate your partner. If this is the case, you should bear in mind that the Dog is also said to store Fire, which may provide you with positive outlets. You are likely to attract submissive partners, but they do not necessarily want to be dominated and so the onus is on you to exercise restraint from time to time. This also means that it will be up to you to suggest spending quality time together, as well as taking responsibility for many other issues.

If you are a weak Wood person, this may not suit you, and you may well find the support and encouragement that you are looking for in a Water person. If you are a strong Wood person and you prefer a more challenging relationship, consider a Metal partner.

Relationships for Yin Wood People

風水

If you have determined that you are a yin Wood person, this section will tell you more about your House of Spouse. Turn first to the section on pages 57–60, which defines the element and animal associated with your birth date. This is your House of Spouse.

Yin Wood people can often attract and be attracted to yang Metal people.

Born on the Day of the Wood Ox

The Ox is associated with the Earth element and, as a Wood person, this element represents your wealth. Since Wood is said to control Earth, this denotes that you may well attract submissive partners but you should keep in mind the fact that the Ox is said to store Metal, so such a relationship may prove more difficult than you imagine.

Of course, this type of relationship may not suit you, especially if your own element is weak, because this form of control would only weaken you further. If you are a weak Wood person, then you may want the loving support that only a Water person can provide, or perhaps you would feel safer in the company of other Wood people. In contrast to this, if your personal element is strong, a Metal person may be what you are looking for, or if you want someone to nurture and nourish, a Fire person may well be ideal, provided they relish this level of support.

Born on the Day of the Wood Rabbit

The Rabbit is associated with the Wood element, indicating that you are attracted to people who are like you and who share the same interests, opinions and ideals. However, this also means that you attract people who may see you as a safe bet and this may not be to your liking.

If your own personal element is fairly weak, this can often be very comforting, but familiarity does not always provide compatibility and this situation can often end in conflict. If your partner is also a Wood person, you will both need to be aware of the hazards of competing against each other, since it is very likely that neither of you will win. If you are a strong Wood person and you are looking for a partner who would provide you with positive outlets for your energy, try a Fire partner, but if you relish and thrive with a challenge, seek out the company of Metal people.

Born on the Day of the Wood Snake

The Snake is associated with the Fire element and this denotes that you tend to devote your energy to support your partners. If this is the case, you should try to conserve your energy as there may be plenty of people who will see you as a meal ticket.

When your own element is strong and you are feeling dynamic, this may not present you with any problems; on the contrary, this may give you the perfect outlet for your energy. However, if your element is weak, this can be very draining and as a result you may find that your partner is too demanding, which may lead to problems. If your personal element is weak, the chances are that a relationship with either a Water person or another Wood person would be far more suitable for you, providing you with the support that you need, rather than a Fire person who will rely on you for support.

Born on the Day of the Wood Sheep

The Sheep is associated with the Earth element, indicating that you are very much in the driving seat, since Wood is said to control Earth. The Sheep is also said to store Wood, so you may well receive more help and support than you acknowledge.

Since the Earth element represents your wealth, you must be careful not to let this aspect dominate your relationship. The fact that your partner is linked in with your finances is not always obvious, but it is important to take this into account. If you are a weak Wood Person, you may find this very depleting, because taking control is probably the last thing you want. If this is the case, a partner belonging to the Water element may well be more appealing.

Born on the Day of the Wood Rooster

The Rooster is associated with the Metal element, indicating that you are attracted to dominant partners.

If your personal element is weak, this type of relationship is likely to leave you feeling exhausted, and a relationship with a Water person would be much more agreeable. If your element is strong, you may benefit from a partner who will push you further, enabling you to achieve even more. If your partner's element is strong, this could be very beneficial for all concerned. However, if your partner's element is weak, it may be that as a strong Wood person you might be more attracted to people belonging to the Fire element, since they allow you to shine and express yourself fully.

Born on the Day of the Wood Pig

The Pig is associated with Water, denoting that you attract and are attracted to partners who regenerate and stimulate you.

Wood is very happy when being fed and supported by Water, but if you are a weak Wood person and your partner is a strong Water person, this may have an adverse effect, resulting in your partner 'drowning' you. If you are a strong Wood person, this type of relationship may not suit you because, instead of seeking support, you may well be looking for someone to care for. In this case, a Fire person may be more fun, since Fire represents the perfect outlet for a strong Wood person. If you prefer the idea of a more challenging relationship, you might enjoy a relationship with a Metal person, who may have the ability to help you transform your life, as long as you are willing for them to do this.

Relationships for Yang Fire People

風水

f you have determined that you are a yang Fire person, this section will tell you more about your House of Spouse. Turn first to the section on pages 57–60 which defines the element and animal associated with your birth date. This is your House of Spouse.

Yang Fire people can often attract and be attracted to yin Metal people.

Born on the Day of the Fire Rat

Since the Rat is associated with the Water element, this combination of Fire and Water can provide a challenging aspect for a Fire person and you may well be attracted to strong partners who are fairly dominant.

If your personal element is strong and your partner likes to be in control, you may find that this works in your favour, but if you are a weak Fire person, you may find this type of relationship very restricted and therefore unsuitable. If this is the case, Wood people may well be much more appealing, because they may provide the type of support and encouragement that you yearn for. If your element is strong but you don't relish challenging relationships, then a partner belonging to the Earth element will allow you to express yourself fully. If their personal element is fairly weak and they would therefore benefit from more Fire, this relationship could be very favourable for all concerned.

Born on the Day of the Fire Tiger

The Tiger is associated with Wood, which may seem heaven-sent for a weak Fire person since Wood generates and feeds Fire. However, it is important to realise that this can result in you becoming too dependent upon your partner so that you deplete their energy unless their element is strong enough to cope.

The negative aspect of this House of Spouse is that you may well attract people who see you merely as an outlet for their energy. If you are a strong Fire person, this will not suit you since they will expect you to be an extension of them. This may result in support and encouragement but it will be very much on their terms. If this is the case, a relationship with an

Earth person may be more suitable for you. On the other hand, if you are attracted to more steamy, challenging relationships, a Water person may just be ideal.

Born on the Day of the Fire Dragon

The Dragon belongs to the Earth element, denoting that you support and nourish your partner, and if your element is strong, then this role in a relationship can be very suitable for you. Of course, this positive side of you must also suit your partner, otherwise you may be in danger of smothering them. Another aspect of the equation, however, is that the Dragon is said to store Water, which may well provide you with the right amount of resistance.

The downside is that you may well attract partners who are looking for someone who will take care of and provide for them. This may not suit you, especially if your own element is weak, because you will be probably happier with someone who will be supportive towards you. In that case, a relationship with a Water person may well bring much greater benefits. If you are a strong Fire person but find the prospect of looking after your partner boring, then a Water person may provide the stimulation you are looking for.

Born on the Day of the Fire Horse

The Horse is associated with Fire, so this denotes that you are a Fire person who attracts and is attracted to other Fire people; in simple terms, you are looking for people who share similar views, hobbies and interests or who have the same outlook on life as you.

If your element is weak, then another Fire person as a partner would provide additional security and comfort, but the negative aspect of this is that you may well tend to play safe and, as a result, be left feeling unfulfilled. If you are a strong Fire person, you may prefer the company of Earth people, who provide a platform for you to perform, allowing you to express yourself fully. Alternatively, you may like the challenging aspects of a Water person or the additional support that a Wood person would provide. Of course, all of these are only favourable if you also provide your partner with what they need: otherwise conflict may well result.

Born on the Day of the Fire Monkey

The Monkey is associated with the Metal element and this denotes that you attract and are attracted to submissive partners. If your element is strong and your partner is happy with this, then it works very well. However, if your partner's element is weak, you may well tend to dominate them, which is unlikely to make them feel fulfilled in the relationship.

If you are a weak Fire person, having a partner who always expects you to take control can be very debilitating and if this is the case a relationship with someone belonging to the Wood element may be much better since they would offer support and encouragement. On the other hand, if your element is strong and you don't like being in control, then a partner belonging to the Earth element would provide you with an opportunity to nourish and rejuvenate them, although of course you will run the risk of feeling your own energies have been depleted from time to time.

Born on the Day of the Fire Dog

The Dog is associated with the Earth element, which indicates that you like to nurture, nourish and support your partner. This works well when your element is strong, but when your element is weak, this can leave you feeling drained. The negative aspect of this House of Spouse is that you may well attract people who see you as an easy touch, someone who will do everything for them.

If your personal element is weak, relationships with Wood people or other Fire people may be appropriate, providing the kind of support that you crave. If you are a strong Fire person looking for a happy, easy life, then this relationship may be ideal, especially if your partner enjoys the level of support that you can offer. The Dog is also associated with the Fire element and this means that your partner does have the ability to support you, so keep this in mind.

Relationships for Yin Fire People

風水

f you have determined that you are a yin Fire person, this section will tell you more about your House of Spouse. Turn first to the section on pages 57–60 which defines the element and animal associated with your birth date. This is your House of Spouse.

Yin Fire people can often attract and be attracted to yang Water people.

Born on the Day of the Fire Ox

The Ox is associated with the Earth element and this House of Spouse will attract strong Fire people who are in need of the Earth element, through which they can express themselves. This combination denotes that you may be vulnerable to people who look to you for support, and you may find it difficult to refuse.

If you are a weak Fire person, you will not find this type of relationship suitable for you as you may be left feeling depleted by the demands of an Earth person, who will look to you for constant support and encouragement. If this is the case, a relationship with a Wood person would probably provide the support and encouragement that you are looking for. If your element is strong but you prefer a more challenging relationship, a Water person may provide the fireworks that you are looking for. Of course, this will only work if it also suits your partner. If not, stand back and watch the explosions!

Born on the Day of the Fire Rabbit

The Rabbit is associated with the Wood element, which denotes that you enjoy support and encouragement from your partner. If you are in a relationship that is not working in that way, the chances are that your partner does not belong to the Wood element.

If you are a weak Fire person and you do not receive this level of support, it is likely that your relationships will leave you feeling flat, especially if your partner belongs to the Water element, which will only extinguish your Fire even further. If your partner is a Wood person and your element is weak, then you must be careful not to deplete your partner's energies;

after all, if you do they will be unable to continue supporting you. If your element is strong, you may resent partners who want to devote themselves to you and if this is the case, you may be attracted to Earth people, who would delight in having you around.

Born on the Day of the Fire Snake

As a Fire person, this House of Spouse denotes that you are attracted to like-minded people but this can also imply that you are attracted to relationships that you consider safe.

This can be very positive, especially if you and your partner are both weak Fire people. However, the negative aspect to relationships of this type is that you often find yourself in competition with your partner. If your element is strong, then you may find that a supportive partner is not very appealing and you may yearn for someone far more challenging, like a Water person, or a partner who provides a positive outlet for your energy, like an Earth person. If you like to be in control, then a Metal person may be the answer, providing of course, that they are happy to let their partner take control, otherwise there may be conflict.

Born on the Day of the Fire Sheep

The Sheep is associated with the Earth element, which means that you like to support and inspire your partner. The Sheep is said to store Wood and this means that you can expect to get support from your partner, although perhaps not as often as you would like.

If you are a strong Fire person, this mutually supportive relationship will work very well but if not, you run the risk of exhaustion. You are also prone to attracting people who are unable to support themselves and if your personal element is weak, you will find this relationship very demanding, in which case the chances are that you would be a lot happier with a Wood person, who would supply the level of support that you crave. If you are a strong Fire person and your partner is a weak Earth person, you may be a little overwhelming and, if this is so, you may need to give your partner a little more space.

Born on the Day of the Fire Rooster

The Rooster is associated with the Metal element, which suggests that you prefer to take charge in your relationships and that you attract people who are suited to this.

Of course, this may not suit you, and if you would prefer your partner to take charge, someone belonging to the Water element would be much more suitable. If your partner is a weak Metal person, then you may have an adverse effect on them and you should try to accept that you can appear very dominating at times. If this is the case, then you will have to take a more sympathetic approach and try to be more encouraging. If you are a strong Fire person looking for additional support, then a Wood person may be just what you are looking for. Alternatively, you could well be very happy with an Earth person on whom you can shower your love, affection and support.

Born on the Day of the Fire Pig

This House of Spouse suggests that you are attracted to challenging relationships or ones in which your partner is very much in control. This may or may not suit you, depending on the strength of your personal element.

If you are a weak Fire person, this may well cause you concern because the chances are you will not relish this type of domination. In that case, you will probably be more attracted to the support and encouragement that a Wood person would provide for you. If your personal element is strong and you are looking for someone to nurture and nourish, then an Earth person may just be what you are looking for, but if you are looking for even more support, then the chances are that a Wood person would be more compatible, providing of course that this arrangement suits them.

Relationships for Yang Earth People

風水

If you have determined that you are a yang Earth person, this section will tell you more about your House of Spouse. Turn first to the section on pages 57–60, which defines the element and animal associated with your birth date. This is your House of Spouse.

Yang Earth people can often attract and be attracted to yin Water people.

Born on the Day of the Earth Rat

Since the Rat is associated with the Water element and Earth is said to control Water, this denotes that you are very much in control when it comes to your relationships. This may suit your partner, but if not, try to encourage rather than dictate: if your partner's element is weak, this approach will pay dividends.

If your element is weak, this type of relationship may not be suitable for you, and you may well prefer the support and encouragement that a Fire person would provide; but if your personal element is strong, perhaps you would relish the challenge that a Wood partner would provide. Water represents wealth to an Earth person and it could be argued that this House of Spouse denotes the fact that your partner is linked to your wealth, in which case it would be wise to remember this, because support comes in many ways and is not always obvious.

Born on the Day of the Earth Tiger

The Tiger is associated with the Wood element, denoting that you may be attracted to people who are much stronger than you, or that you attract people who want to dominate you.

In either case, this is unlikely to suit you if your personal element is weak. If it is support and encouragement you are looking for, then a Fire person may be ideal, provided their element is strong, otherwise you may well deplete their energies, in which case the relationship may not last. If you are a strong Earth person who is looking for a positive outlet, then someone belonging to the Metal element, on whom you could lavish your attention, may just be what you need. It is essential, however, that your partner thrives on this level of support, otherwise you may be in danger of smothering them and being more like a mother than a lover.

Born on the Day of the Earth Dragon

Since the Dragon is also associated with the Earth element, this denotes a 'pure pillar', indicating that you attract and are attracted to partners who share a similar outlook on life. This can be a blessing, especially if you are looking for mutual support and encouragement, because these types of relationships are often very safe. On the negative side, however, they can result in you having to compete with your partner.

For some Earth people this will be very unattractive, especially if your personal element is very strong and you are really seeking outlets for your energy. If this sounds like you, look for a Metal person on whom to lavish your attention. On the other hand, if your personal element is weak, a Fire person who wants to protect you may provide you with the loving care and support that you dream of.

Born on the Day of the Earth Horse

The Horse is associated with the Fire element, which nourishes and replenishes Earth, so you will attract the nurturing type.

If you are a weak Earth person, finding someone who is willing to lavish their attention on you may well be ideal, as long as their element is strong. The negative side to this relationship is that you have a tendency to drain your partner's energy. If their element is weak, this may well cause conflict and it would be beneficial to try to be less demanding. After all, if you deplete your partner's energy, who will support you? If your personal element is very strong, additional support may well be the last thing you need, in which case a Wood person is more likely to provide the challenge you need, while a Metal person would happily absorb your love and affection.

Born on the Day of the Earth Monkey

The Monkey is associated with the Metal element and this House of Spouse combination may leave you feeling exhausted and unable to find the strength to follow through relationships, especially if your personal element is weak.

If you are a weak Earth person, you may prefer a partner who regenerates and inspires you. In this case, a Fire person would be a very attractive proposition because the chances are that they will provide you with the kind of loving support that you crave. If your personal element is strong and you are looking for a positive outlet for your energy, then you will probably not appreciate a supportive partner, preferring instead someone who will provide you with a challenge, such as a Wood person. Alternatively, perhaps you would prefer an easier relationship, which a Metal person would be likely to offer you.

Born on the Day of the Earth Dog

Since the Dog is associated with the Earth element, this is another 'pure pillar', denoting that you are attracted to the company of other like-minded people. If your partner feels the same way, this can be very beneficial for both of you. This is not always the case, however, and in a worst-case scenario, this can lead to competition between the two of you.

If you are looking for something more stimulating, you may prefer the company of Fire people, who offer you the support and encouragement that you need. However, since the Dog is also said to store Fire, another Earth person may also make a good partner for you. If you like to be in control in your relationships, you should be looking for a Water person; however, it is important that they are also happy with this balance in the relationship or you will be in danger of completely overwhelming them.

Relationships for Yin Earth People

風水

f you have determined that you are a yin Earth person, this section will tell you more about your House of Spouse. Turn first to the section on pages 57–60, which defines the element and animal associated with your birth date. This is your House of Spouse.

Yin Earth people often attract and are attracted to yang Wood people.

Born on the Day of the Earth Ox

Since the Ox is associated with the Earth element, this House of Spouse denotes that you attract and are attracted to people with whom you have a lot in common and share similar interests and beliefs.

If both you and your partner are weak Earth people, this relationship can work well, since you will be able to support and encourage each other, but if you are lacking support and encouragement, perhaps you would feel happier in the company of Fire people. If your personal element is strong, this type of relationship may not be very attractive and you would be more likely to find happiness with a Metal person on whom you could lavish your attention - always assuming that they want that level of attention. Alternatively, you may prefer a Wood person who would offer you the kind of challenge that you may relish.

Born on the Day of the Earth Rabbit

The Rabbit is associated with the Wood element and, since Wood is said to control Earth, this denotes that you are attracted to people who are very much in control. This may not always be beneficial for you, however, especially if you are a weak Earth person, because your partner could demoralise you rather than stimulate you, even if that is not their intention.

If you are a weak Earth person, you may be attracted to Fire people, who have the ability to regenerate and inspire Earth people, or you may feel more secure with other Earth people with whom you share a lot in common. Alternatively, you may prefer taking the lead in relationships, in which case a relationship with a Water person may be more to your liking; provided that this suits your partner, this could be a good match.

Born on the Day of the Earth Snake

The element of the Snake is Fire, indicating that you are likely to attract Fire people, and for many Earth people this offers an ideal relationship, especially if they flourish with the unique level of support that a Fire person can offer. Given your Earth element, however, you have the potential to drain your partner's energy, so bear this in mind and try not to be too demanding.

However idyllic this partnership may sound, it will not be attractive for all Earth people: strong Earth people in particular may prefer the company of Wood people who would provide them with a much more challenging relationship. Alternatively, as a strong Earth person, you may benefit from a relationship with a Metal person, who would provide you with a positive outlet for your energy, especially if their personal element is weak, since they would no doubt appreciate your strength of character.

Born on the Day of the Earth Sheep

The Sheep is associated with the Earth element, giving a double dose of Earth energies, so you will be attracted to others of the same element. This type of relationship can be mutually supportive, but the negative aspects suggest that you may find yourself having to compete with your partner and, since the Sheep is also associated with the Wood element, this may prove difficult for you.

If you are a weak Earth person, combining with another Earth person may not suit you, especially if your partner's element is strong, because you may resent having to support them. You would be better advised to look for the company of Fire people, who are able to rejuvenate and inspire you. If you are a strong Earth person and you prefer to be the one who takes the initiative when it comes to relationships, a Water person may be the soul-mate you are searching for, provided that they are happy to let their partner take control.

Born on the Day of the Earth Rooster

The Rooster is associated with the Metal element, indicating that you like to spoil and pamper your partner; if your element is strong and your partner responds favourably to your efforts, this can result in a very happy and harmonious relationship.

Of course, this is not always the case and if you are a weak Earth person, this can have a very depleting effect on you. Coupled with the fact that you may attract others who are looking for someone who will look after them, this may leave you feeling very disillusioned and exhausted. The remedy in this situation is to find someone who will support and encourage you and if this is what you are looking for, try to establish a relationship with a Fire person. If you are a strong Earth person who is looking for a challenge in life, then perhaps you should consider a Wood partner, but if you are looking for an easy life, then a Metal person would be more suitable.

Born on the Day of the Earth Pig

The Pig is associated with the Water element and, since Earth is said to control Water, this House of Spouse denotes that when it comes to relationships, you are very much in the driving seat. So keep this in mind and try to encourage your partner, rather than making too many demands.

This may not be your style, and if your personal element is weak, then having a partner who expects you to take charge all the time may leave you feeling frustrated. If this is the case, another Earth person may be more attractive. If it is support and encouragement that you are looking for, then you would do well to consider a Fire person, who has the ability to regenerate, motivate and encourage you. If you are a strong Earth person looking for a challenge, consider a Wood person, but keep in mind that unless they need your Earth qualities, this combination could become explosive.

Relationships for Yang Metal People

風水

I
f you have determined that you are a yang Metal person, this section will tell you more about your House of Spouse. Turn first to the section on pages 57–60, which defines the element and animal associated with your birth date. This is your House of Spouse.

Yang Metal people often attract and are attracted to yin Wood people.

Born on the Day of the Metal Rat

Since the Rat is associated with the Water element, this House of Spouse denotes that you tend to support and encourage your partners. This can be very harmonious and beneficial for all concerned, providing your element is strong and your partner's element is in need of strengthening, but if it is not, this can often lead to problems.

If your personal element is weak, a relationship in which you are nurturing and encouraging your partner to a large degree will leave you feeling depleted. In addition, if your partner's element is strong, then you may run the risk of being over-protective, which may not suit your partner as they may not appreciate the level of support you try to offer. In this case, an Earth person may be much more suited to you, providing you with the support and encouragement you need. As a strong Metal person, a Fire person may provide you with an attractive challenge to prevent boredom from setting in.

Born on the Day of the Metal Tiger

The Tiger represents the Wood element and, for a Metal person, this denotes that you take the leading role where relationships are concerned and that you attract others who are more than happy for you to do that.

This may not suit everyone, because if your partner's element is weak you may seem to be too dominating. If you are in this kind of relationship, try to give your partner the space they need, otherwise you run the risk of driving them away. If your personal element is weak, it is likely that you would much rather be supported and encouraged by your partner than be in control; in this case, an Earth person would be a good partner for you. If you are a strong Metal person, a Fire person would add spice to your life, or a Water person would enjoy the attention you could lavish on them.

Born on the Day of the Metal Dragon

The Dragon's Earth can often be just the tonic that a Metal person needs, especially a weak one, and this House of Spouse denotes that you are attracted to those who can regenerate, rejuvenate and inspire you. The negative aspect of this is that you also have the ability to attract those who see you as an outlet for their own energies.

If you are a strong Metal person, this may not suit you and you should look for a more challenging relationship with a Fire person. If you like to take the initiative in your relationships, then look for a Wood person, as long as your partner is happy for you to take charge. If your personal element is strong and you relish a partner who will push you to your limits, a Fire person may well provide the spark that you need to transform your life.

Born on the Day of the Metal Horse

If you are a weak Metal person, having the Horse in your House of Spouse may not be to your liking, because the Horse is associated with the Fire element and indicates that you are likely to attract people who prefer to dominate their partners.

A weak Metal person is likely to be attracted to Earth people because they can offer you the support and inspiration you need. If your personal element is strong and you are both happy for your partner to take the lead, you can be very harmonious with a Fire partner. However, as a strong Metal person you may also be attracted to Water people, since they provide the perfect outlet for your energy, offering you the ideal opportunity for you to shine and to express yourself fully. If it is support and encouragement that you are after, then you may well flourish and prosper in the company of Earth people, who have the ability to offer you this kind of relationship.

Born on the Day of the Metal Monkey

As the Monkey is associated with the Metal element, this denotes that you are attracted to like-minded people; if your partner and you are both weak Metal people, this may well provide you both with the support and encouragement you need.

If your partner and you are both strong Metal people, the chances are that you will compete with each other, something that may not be acceptable to either of you. As a strong Metal person, you may feel more comfortable in the company of Water people, who will allow you to express yourself freely, or Fire people, who will provide you with a challenge. On the other hand, if your element is strong and you like to be in command, then a Wood partner may work very well, provided of course that they are happy for you to dictate the terms of the relationship.

Born on the Day of the Metal Dog

Since the Dog is associated with the Earth element, this combination is ideal for a weak Metal person, as it indicates that they are likely to attract a partner who will offer them support and encouragement. If your partner is a strong Earth person, then this would work very well for all concerned, but if they are not, then you may well drain your partner's energy at times. If this happens, you may need to exercise caution: since the Dog is also associated with the Fire element, they may well fight back.

For some people, especially strong Metal people who are not really in need of support, this arrangement holds very little appeal and they may therefore relish something more challenging. Alternatively, if you are a fairly dominant person, then a relationship with a Wood person may be more suitable for you, but this will only work if your partner is happy with this and that their personal element is strong enough to cope.

Relationships for Yin Metal People

風水

f you have determined that you are a yin Metal person, this section will tell you more about your House of Spouse. Turn first to the section on pages 57–60, which defines the element and animal associated with your birth date. This is your House of Spouse.

Yin Metal people often attract and are attracted to yang Fire people.

Born on the Day of the Metal Ox

The Ox is associated with the Earth element, which regenerates and encourages Metal, denoting that you are attracted to partners who can do the same for you.

If you are a weak Metal person, a relationship with someone who supports you may just be what you are after, but if you are a strong Metal person, this may not be the case. Compatibility is all about both partners getting what they need and if you are a strong Metal person, then support is probably not top of your agenda and you may be much more attracted to relationships involving Water people, to whom you could devote your energy. Of course, this will only really work if this also suits your partner, otherwise you may well be in danger of smothering them. If you are a strong Metal person who likes to be in control, then a Wood partner might just be perfect, but if you prefer something more stimulating, perhaps you would relish the challenge provided only by a Fire person.

Born on the Day of the Metal Rabbit

Since the Rabbit is associated with the Wood element, this House of Spouse denotes that you like to be in charge, at least as far as your relationships are concerned. The negative aspects of this suggest that you also attract people who are looking for someone like you to take charge of their life, and if this is not your style, you may want something different.

If you are a weak Metal person, you may appreciate having a partner who will regenerate, support and inspire you and find your soul-mate in the form of an Earth person. If you are a strong Metal person, you may be attracted to Fire people, who would provide you with a challenge. If you would be happy with someone on whom you could lavish your attention, a Water person may be ideal, providing of course that they respond favourably to your efforts.

Born on the Day of the Metal Snake

The Snake is associated with the Fire element, which for Metal people provides quite a challenge, as they will attract partners who may try to dominate them.

If you are a weak Metal person, then this is far from ideal, because the chances are that what you really want is support; in this case another Metal person or an Earth person may make a much more favourable partner. However, if you are a strong Metal person, support and encouragement may not be enough and you may want something more challenging, in which case a Fire person might be just the thing to spice up your life. If you are a strong Metal person and you are looking for someone to lavish your attention on, search out a Water person who is in need of that kind of relationship.

Born on the Day of the Metal Sheep

The Sheep is associated with the Earth element and since Earth is said to generate Metal, this denotes that you are attracted to those who can support and encourage you.

This sounds a very attractive proposition, but if you are a strong Metal person, it is probably not what turns you on and you may feel that your partner is smothering you. If your personal element is strong and you are a fairly dominant person, then a Wood partner may be more suitable, as long as they thrive with a powerful partner. If you are a weak Metal person, an Earth partner may be ideal, providing you with all the loving support that you crave, although you should bear in mind that you also have the ability to deplete your partner from time to time, so try to be a little less dependent.

Born on the Day of the Metal Rooster

Since the Rooster is associated with the Metal element, you attract and are attracted to people who share similar views and interests.

If you and your partner are both weak Metal people, this relationship may work very well for both of you, because you are likely to support and encourage each other. Having a partner just like you may suit some people, but for others this type of relationship is not particularly attractive, especially if their personal element is strong. Some people naturally relish a challenge in life and if this is you, then look no further than a Fire person, who will certainly provide the spark you are looking for. If you crave the attention of a partner who will lavish support and encouragement on you, then you are likely to prefer the company of Earth people, who have the ability to rejuvenate and replenish Metal.

Born on the Day of the Metal Pig

As a Metal person, this House of Spouse denotes that you may be left feeling drained and exhausted in your relationships, especially if you are a weak Metal person, because the Pig is associated with Water, which can deplete Metal.

If you are a strong Metal person, this should not present a problem, and if your partner flourishes and prospers with your support, then you should both benefit. However, if you are a weak Metal person, a partner belonging to the Earth element would be more likely to provide you with the support you need. Some people are attracted to dominant partners while others prefer to be in command, and if you like taking the initiative in your relationships, you should try a Wood person – as long as this also suits them. If your element is strong and you relish a challenge, then perhaps you would thrive with a Fire person.

Calculating the Fate Cycles
風水

The final layer of consideration, when looking at your personal energies in relation to those around you, is the vital element of timing. Everyone is aware that sometimes life tends to go more smoothly than at other times. With feng shui, you can calculate when those times are likely to be, and act accordingly. That means you should be able to maximise the benefits of positive energies and minimise the effects of the negative energies.

Using the calculations we made to determine your pillars, we can calculate an individual's fate cycles or luck pillars. These represent phases of ten years and allow us to identify what phase we are in at any given time and to determine whether or not it is favourable.

To make these calculations, you will need the information on pages 59–60.

Step 1: Identify the person's month pillar and the number allocated to that pillar in the table on pages 59–60.

Step 2: Identify the person's year pillar and whether that year is yin or yang. Note whether they are male or female.

Step 3: Decide whether the progression is yang (forward) or yin (backward).

For males (yang) born in a year with a yang year pillar, use a yang progression (forwards).

For males (yang) born in a year with a yin year pillar, use a yin progression (backwards).

For females (yin) born in a year with a yang year pillar, use a yin progression (backwards).

For females (yin) born in a year with a yin year pillar, use a yang progression (forwards)

In other words, yin/yin and yang/yang combinations use a yang progression (forwards); yin/yang or yang/yin use a yin progression (backwards).

Step 4: Using the appropriate progression, the first luck pillar is the one after the month pillar, and so on.

Notice that the cycles alternate between yin and yang.

Example 1: Finding the luck pillars for a man born in the month of the yang Metal Monkey, in the year of the yin Water Pig

Step 1: His month pillar is the yang Metal Monkey, which is number 57 in the table.

Step 2: His year pillar is yin Water Pig and he is male.

Step 3: A male (yang) born in a yin year has a yin (backward) progression.

Step 4: The first luck pillar is the one after the month pillar (57) in a yin progression and is therefore 56, Earth Sheep, then 55 Earth Horse, then 54 Fire Snake, then 53 Fire Dragon, and so on.

1ST CYCLE	2ND CYCLE	3RD CYCLE	4TH CYCLE	5TH CYCLE	6TH CYCLE
Yin Earth	Yang Earth	Yin Fire	Yang Fire	Yin Wood	Yang Wood
Sheep	Horse	Snake	Dragon	Rabbit	Tiger

Example 2: Finding the luck pillars for a woman born in the month of the yang Metal Monkey, in the year of the yin Water Pig

Step 1: Her month pillar is the yang Metal Monkey, which is number 57 in the table.

Step 2: Her year pillar is the yin Water Pig and she is female.

Step 3: A female (yin) born in a yin year has a yang (forward) progression.

Step 4: The first luck pillar is the one after the month pillar (57) in a yang progression and is therefore 58 Metal Rooster, then 59 Water Dog, then 60 Water Pig, then 1 Wood Rat, then 2 Wood Ox, and so on.

1ST CYCLE	2ND CYCLE	3RD CYCLE	4TH CYCLE	5TH CYCLE	6TH CYCLE
Yin Metal	Yang Water	Yin Water	Yang Wood	Yin Wood	Yin Fire
Rooster	Dog	Pig	Rat	Ox	Tiger

Calculating the Age at which the Fate Cycles Begin

Each of these luck pillars represents a specific year and these are defined by the actual birth date in relation to the month. If the fate cycles move in a yang (forward) progression, count the number of days from the birthday to the start of the next Chinese month. If the fate cycles move in a yin (backward) progression, count the number of days from the birthday back to the beginning of that Chinese month.

Step 1: Note the hour, day, month and year pillars and work out the fate cycles as before.

Step 2: Determine whether the progression is yang (forward) or yin (backward).

Step 3: Look at the table of Chinese months on page 63.

Step 4: Count backwards or forwards from the birthday to the end of the month and note the number of days.

Step 5: Each day represents four months. Calculate the number of years this represents and round up to the nearest year.

Step 6: The first fate cycle is said to begin when the person is that number of years old, and the rest follow in ten-year cycles.

Example 1: Finding the fate cycles of a woman born at 3.30 pm on 16 May 1963

Step 1: Work out the fate cycles from the information in the table below:

HOUR PILLAR	DAY PILLAR	MONTH PILLAR	YEAR PILLAR
Yang Water	Yin Earth	Yin Fire	Yin Water
Monkey	Sheep	Snake	Rabbit

1ST CYCLE	2ND CYCLE	3RD CYCLE	4TH CYCLE	5TH CYCLE	6TH CYCLE
Yin Metal	Yang Water	Yin Water	Yang Wood	Yin Wood	Yin Fire
Rooster	Dog	Pig	Rat	Ox	Tiger

Step 2: For a woman (yin) born in a yin year, the progression is yang (forward).

Step 3: She was born in the month of the Snake and the next month is the month of the Horse.

Step 4: Count forwards from 16 May to 6 June, the beginning of the month of the Horse. This is 21 days.

Step 5: 21 days represents seven years, to the nearest year.

Step 6: The woman's first fate cycle begins at the age of seven.

AGE 7 (1970)	AGE 17 (1980)	AGE 27 (1990)	AGE 37 (2000)	AGE 47 (2010)	AGE 57 (2020)
Yang Earth	Yin Earth	Yang Metal	Yin Metal	Yang Water	Yin Water
Horse	Sheep	Monkey	Rooster	Dog	Pig

Example 2: Finding the fate cycles of a woman born at 9.30 pm on 18 February 1958

Step 1: Work out the fate cycles from the information as follows.

HOUR PILLAR	DAY PILLAR	MONTH PILLAR	YEAR PILLAR
Yin Earth	Yang Fire	Yang Wood	Yang Earth
Pig	Tiger	Tiger	Dog

1ST CYCLE	2ND CYCLE	3RD CYCLE	4TH CYCLE	5TH CYCLE	6TH CYCLE
Yin Water	Yang Water	Yin Metal	Yang Metal	Yin Earth	Yang Earth
Ox	Rat	Pig	Dog	Rooster	Monkey

Step 2: For a woman (yin) born in a yang year, the progression is yin (backward).

Step 3: She was born in the month of the Tiger and the previous month is the month of the Ox.

Step 4: Count backwards from 18 February to 4 February, the end of the month of the Ox. This is 13 days.

Step 5: 13 days represents five years, to the nearest year.

Step 6: The woman's first fate cycle begins at the age of five.

AGE 5 (1963)	AGE 15 (1973)	AGE 25 (1983)	AGE 35 (1993)	AGE 45 (2003)	AGE 55 (2013)
Yin Water	Yang Water	Yin Metal	Yang Metal	Yin Earth	Yang Earth
Ox	Rat	Pig	Dog	Rooster	Monkey

How to Use Your Fate Cycles
風水

E valuating the strength of the day pillar is the key to using your knowledge of your fate cycles, or luck pillars. Favourable elements can be transformed into directions, colours, shapes and form and by introducing these into our lives, we can enhance our good luck and diminish our bad luck.

If we are in a 'good luck' phase, then we can afford to be more optimistic and more speculative, wealth is easier to create, and we are far more likely to succeed in gaining what we want, whether that is status, recognition, or whatever. In a 'bad luck' pillar, these things are much more difficult to achieve, so it is far more constructive to focus our efforts on conserving our resources and consolidating our position, rather than trying to expand. The Chinese believe that in a good luck cycle we tend to make good judgements and in a bad luck cycle, our judgement is often impaired. The key then is to make the most from our favourable periods when they do occur and to lower our expectations at times when fortune is less favourable. It is all about being in harmony with the energies around us.

To use the luck pillars effectively, you need to identify your personal element and luck pillars, then use the principles of feng shui to adjust the balance of the elements, strengthening those that are weak. This chapter will give you examples of how to do this so that you can put the principles into practice in your own life. Of necessity, it is a basic introduction – feng shui masters take many years' study to achieve their level of knowledge – but it should be sufficient to allow you to change your life, and those of the people around you.

Let us look at one final example, in order to see how we can apply this system to individuals.

Using Your Luck Pillars

This example will help you to understand how to put all this information into practice. It examines the situation with relevance to a woman born at 10.30 pm on 13 September 1972. In the chart overleaf, we can see her four pillars, with the hidden stems in place:

AGE 2 (1974)	AGE 12 (1984)	AGE 22 (1994)	AGE 32 (2004)	AGE 42 (2014)	AGE 52 (2024)
Yang Earth	Yin Fire	Yang Fire	Yin Wood	Yang Wood	Yin Water
Monkey	Sheep	Horse	Snake	Dragon	Rabbit
HIDDEN STEMS	HIDDEN STEMS	HIDDEN STEMS	HIDDEN STEMS	HIDDEN STEMS	HIDDEN STEMS
Yang Metal	Yin Earth	Yin Fire	Yang Fire	Yang Earth	Yin Wood
Yang Water	Yin Fire	Yin Earth	Yang Metal	Yin Wood	
Yang Earth	Yin Wood		Yang Earth	Yin Water	

HOUR PILLAR	DAY PILLAR	MONTH PILLAR	YEAR PILLAR
Yin Metal	Yin Fire	Yin Earth	Yang Water
Pig	Sheep	Rooster	Rat
HIDDEN STEMS	HIDDEN STEMS	HIDDEN STEMS	HIDDEN STEMS
Yang Water	Yin Earth	Yin Metal	Yin Water
Yang Wood	Yin Fire		
	Yin Wood		

The day master indicates that she is a yin Fire person, and the month pillar indicates that she was born in autumn, in the season of the Rooster. Autumn is the season of Metal, so any Metal stems in her chart will be strong. Since Metal is said to generate Water, Water stems will also be fairly strong. Wood is at its weakest during this time, Earth is reasonably strong, but Fire is getting weaker.

She has ten stems in her four pillars: seven major stems and three minor stems, not including the day stem. Three of the major stems are Water, which is said to control Fire; two of the major stems are Earth, which is said to absorb Fire; the other two major stems are Metal, which also weakens Fire, because although Fire controls Metal, Fire is weakened in the process.

It is therefore not difficult to see that Fire is very weak in this chart and therefore this woman is a weak Fire person and would benefit both from more Fire in the elemental balance – because this would provide her with support – and also more Wood – because Wood generates Fire and helps to absorb Water. Anything else would only weaken her personal element even further.

Looking at her fate cycles, or luck pillars, we can see that the cycle in operation from 1994 to 2003 is represented as the yang Fire Horse. As a weak Fire person, this is very good news because her present luck pillar contains favourable elements and she is therefore in a good luck cycle. Some years within that cycle will be better than others, and these can be determined by taking into account the influence of the individual years. For example, 2001 is the year of the yin Metal Snake and 2002 is the year of the yang Water Horse. By comparing these to the fate cycles, we can see if the elements help or hinder them. If the elements in the luck pillar are favourable but the elements associated with the year control those elements, then the good luck is hindered. If the elements in the luck pillar are unfavourable and the elements associated with the year control those elements, then the bad luck is kept under control. For example, a weak Wood person in a luck pillar associated with Water would be in a good period, since Water generates Wood. Within that luck pillar, years associated with Metal, which generates Water, would be good, whereas years associated with Earth, which controls Water, would not.

Maximising Opportunities

The Chinese believe that the measure of success is how well we do during the bad times, not the good times, since it is relatively easy to enjoy life and be nice to others when things are going well.

We therefore need to learn to understand and control the elements at any given time. Balance is the key. When we are weak, we need to strengthen ourselves; when we are strong, we need to flow in order to find a positive outlet and be productive. Opportunities for controlling wealth, power and status are all easier when our personal element is strong. If we strive too hard when our personal element is weak, we run the risk of depleting our own energies.

Wealth, power and status are represented by the element that controls our personal element. For a Wood person, for example, power and status are represented as Metal, since Metal controls Wood. If the Wood is strong, Metal can shape Wood into something useful, but if the Wood is weak, Metal will destroy it. If we overcome the obstacles and challenges in our path, this can enable us to grow and therefore reap the benefits.

Index

風水

adversity, overcoming 8, 75
ancestors 14

back door (sitting direction) 14–15, 33
bagua (pa kua) mirrors 15, 46
bedroom 14, 15
business
  activating your 39, 51
  elements
  and premises 53
  supporting and generating 54
  type of business 51–2
  influence of eight houses 48–50
  moving into new premises 41
  simple changes at work 39–40
  trigrams and 48

ch'i 9, 15, 18, 47, see also yin, yang
Chinese copper coins 16
chueh ming (broken or severed fate) 20,
  25, 49, 73
  see also house, direction and portents
clutter 15, 40
colours 12, 28, 32
compass directions 12, 24–6

day pillar 55–60, 117–18
deities 15

Earth Dog 139
Earth Dragon 138
Earth energy 9, 10–12, 14, 52
Earth female 90, 110
Earth Horse 138
Earth male 90, 110
Earth Monkey 138–9
Earth Ox 140
Earth people at home 73–4, 90–4
Earth people at work 110
  premises facing north 111
  premises facing south 110–11
  premises facing south-east or east 112
  premises facing south-west or
    north-east 111
  premises facing west or north-west 111
Earth Pig 142
Earth Rabbit 140
Earth Rat 137
Earth Rooster 141-2
Earth Sheep 141
Earth Snake 141
earth shrines 15–16
Earth Tiger 137–8
east 24
Eight Characters 117
elements 9–12
  as classification 11–12
  and colour 12
  and compass direction 12

controlling 73–4
destructive cycle 10, 25
effect of seasons 69–70
generative cycle 10, 25
introducing in home 11, 74
and portents in home 24–6
in relation to yin and yang 11
and season 12
and shape 12
units of time 56
your seasonal 69–72
see also business, elements; personal
  element; pillars of destiny
Emperor's Palace 13–14, 18

Facing or Water Star 33, 35
fate periods (cycles) 149–52
  decision-making 41, 153
  how to use your 153–5
  and luck phases 153
  maximising opportunities 155
feng shui 7, 9, 13, 15, 74
Fire Dog 133
Fire Dragon 132
Fire energy 9, 10–12, 52
Fire female 85, 107
Fire Horse 132
Fire male 85, 107
Fire Ox 134
Fire Monkey 132–3
Fire people at home 73–4, 85–9
Fire people at work 107
  premises facing north 108–9
  premises south 107–8
  premises south-east or east 109
  premises facing south-west or
    north-east 108
  premises facing west or north-west 108
Fire Pig 136
Fire Rat 131
Fire Rabbit 134–5
Fire Rooster 135–6
Fire Sheep 135
Fire Snake 135
Fire Tiger 131–2
fish symbol 16
five blessings 16
five rats chasing the clock 66
five tigers chasing the month 64
Flying Star feng shui 14, 27–38
  birth chart of house 27–32
  Former Heaven Arrangement 46–7
  interaction with portents 32
  Later Heaven Arrangement 28
  see also 24 Mountain Stars
Form School feng shui 14
Former Heaven Sequence (Arrangement)
  24, 46–7
front door (facing direction) 14–15, 33

fu wei (bowing to the throne) 19, 26, 49
  see also house, direction and portents

garden 15–16
going with the flow 9

hai huo (accidents and mishaps) 19, 49
  see also house, direction and portents
Heaven, influence of 9, 14
hexagram 42
hidden stems 71–2
home
  earth shrines 15–16
  following the Emperor 13–14
  introducing elements into 11, 74
  purpose of feng shui 13
  simple improvements 14–15
  traditional Chinese symbols 16–17
  see also house
hour pillar 65–6
house
  birth chart 27–31
  odd-shaped 25–6
  see also house, direction and portents;
    period
house, direction and portents
  facing east 22, 25
  facing north 22, 25
  facing north-east 22, 25
  facing north-west 21, 25
  facing south 20
  facing south-east 23, 25
  facing south-west 21, 25
  facing west 21

House of Spouse 56, 116–18, see also
  relationships

Later Heaven Sequence (Arrangement) 24,
  27, 28, 47–8
lighting 15, 39–40
liu sha (six curses, six imps) 19, 49
  see also house, direction and portents
lo shu (Magic Square) 24, 27
luck 8, 41, see also fate periods

Magic Square (lo shu) 24, 27
Metal Dog 145
Metal Dragon 144
Metal energy 9, 10–12, 52
Metal female 95, 113
Metal Horse 144
Metal male 95, 113
Metal Monkey 144–5
Metal Ox 146
Metal people at home 73–4, 95–9
Metal people at work 113
  premises facing north 114–15
  premises facing south 113–14
  premises facing south-east or east 115
  premises facing south-west or
    north-east 114
  premises facing west or north-west 114
Metal Pig 148
Metal Rabbit 146
Metal Rat 143
Metal Rooster 147–8
Metal Sheep 147

Metal Snake 147
Metal Tiger 143–4
month pillar 63–4
24 Mountain Stars 33–4
  applied to your home 35–8
  and compass direction 33
  flight path of 34–5
  name and direction 34
  typical chart 36

nien yen (long life) 18, 49
  see also house, direction and portents
nine chambers 13, 14
north 24
north, north-east/north-west 24

offices 40

pa kua (bagua) mirrors 15, 46
peace symbol 16
period number
  colour and luck 32
  and flying star 28, 32
  period 1 to 3 houses 29
  period 4 to 6 houses 30
  period 7 to 9 houses 31
Period Star (number) 28, 35–6
personal element
  calculating see pillars of destiny
  Chinese seasons 69–70
  hidden stems 71–2
  and relationships 117–18
  strength 69–72
pillar table 57, 60
pillars of destiny 55–6
  constructing chart 67–8
  day pillar 55–6, 57–60
  hour pillar 65–6
  month pillar 63–4
  pillar table 57, 60
  and relationships 116–17
  year pillar 61–2
  see also day pillar, year pillar
portents 20–2
  at workplace 48–50
  description 18–19
  and elements in home 24–6
  see also specific portents
purity, symbol of 17

relationships 116–18, see also yin and yang
  people

seasons
  at time of birth 70
  effect on elements 12, 69–70
shapes, according to elements 12
sheng ch'i (source of ch'i) 18–19, 25, 32,
  49, 73–4
  see also house, direction and portents
shop windows 40
Sitting or Mountain Star 33, 35
south, south-east/-west 24
symbols 16–17

Ten Thousand Year Calendar 55–6
t'ien i (t'ien yi, heavenly doctor) 19, 49
  see also house, direction and portents

time 56
time cycles 28
toilet seat down 14
trigrams 42–5, 46–9

Water Dog 121
Water Dragon 120
Water energy 9, 10–12, 52
Water female 75, 101
Water Horse 120
Water male 75, 101
Water Monkey 120
Water Ox 122
Water people at home 73–4, 75–8
Water Pig 124
Water Rabbit 122
Water Rat 119
Water Rooster 123
Water Sheep 123
Water Snake 123
Water Tiger 119
wealth, lucky symbols 16
west 24
windows 15, 40
Wood Dog 127
Wood Dragon 126
Wood energy 9, 10–12, 52
Wood female 80, 104
Wood Horse 126
Wood male 80, 104
Wood Monkey 126
Wood people at home 73–4, 80–4
Wood people at work
    elemental chart 104
    premises facing north 106
    premises facing south 104–5
    premises facing south-east or east 106
    premises facing south-west or
        north-east 105
    premises facing west or north-west 105
Wood Ox 128
Wood Pig 130
Wood Rabbit 128
Wood Rooster 129
Wood Sheep 129
Wood Snake 129
Wood Rat 125
Wood Tiger 125
working at home 40
wu kuei (five ghosts) 19, 49
    see also house, direction and portents

yang Earth people, relationships
    born on day of Earth Dog 139
    born on day of Earth Dragon 138
    born on day of Earth Horse 138
    born on day of Earth Monkey 138–9
    born on day of Earth Rat 137
    born on day of Earth Tiger 137–8
yang Fire people, relationships
    born on day of Fire Dog 133
    born on day of Fire Dragon 132
    born on day of Fire Horse 132
    born on day of Fire Monkey 132–3
    born on day of Fire Rat 131
    born on day of Fire Tiger 131–2

yang Metal people, relationships
    born on day of Metal Dog 145
    born on day of Metal Dragon 144
    born on day of Metal Horse 144
    born on day of Metal Monkey 144–5
    born on day of Metal Rat 143
    born on day of Metal Tiger 143–4
yang Water people, relationships
    born on day of Water Dog 121
    born on day of Water Dragon 120
    born on day of Water Horse 120
    born on day of Water Monkey 120
    born on day of Water Rat 119
    born on day of Water Tiger 119
yang Wood people, relationships
    born on day of Wood Dog 127
    born on day of Wood Dragon 126
    born on day of Wood Horse 126
    born on day of Wood Monkey 126
    born on day of Wood Rat 125
    born on day of Wood Tiger 125
year pillar 61–2
yin, yang 9, 11, 15, see also feng shui
    24 Mountain Stars 33, 35
    at home 14–15
    and Former Heaven Sequence 47
    and personal element 56, 57
    and trigrams 42
    in workplace 39–40
yin Earth people, relationships
    born on day of Earth Ox 140
    born on day of Earth Pig 142
    born on day of Earth Rabbit 140
    born on day of Earth Rooster 141–2
    born on day of Earth Sheep 141
    born on day of Earth Snake 141
yin Fire people, relationships
    born on day of Fire Ox 134
    born on day of Fire Pig 136
    born on day of Fire Rabbit 134–5
    born on day of Fire Rooster 135–6
    born on day of Fire Sheep 135
    born on day of Fire Snake 135
yin Metal people, relationships
    born on day of Metal Ox 146
    born on day of Metal Pig 148
    born on day of Metal Rabbit 146–7
    born on day of Metal Rooster 147–8
    born on day of Metal Sheep 147
    born on day of Metal Snake 147
yin Water people, relationships
    born on day of Water Ox 122
    born on day of Water Pig 124
    born on day of Water Rabbit 122
    born on day of Water Rooster 123
    born on day of Water Sheep 123
    born on day of Water Snake 123
yin Wood people, relationships
    born on day of Wood Ox 128
    born on day of Wood Pig 130
    born on day of Wood Rabbit 128–9
    born on day of Wood Rooster 129
    born on day of Wood Sheep 129
    born on day of Wood Snake 129